Retro Recipes from the '50s and '60s

Also in This Series

Retro Recipes from the '50s and '60s

103 Vintage Appetizers, Dinners, and Drinks Everyone Will Love

Addie Gundry

St. Martin's Griffin ✵ New York

RETRO RECIPES FROM THE '50S AND '60S. Text and photography © 2017
Prime Publishing LLC. All rights reserved. Printed in the United States of America.
For information, address St. Martin's Press, 175 Fifth Avenue, New York, N.Y. 10010.

www.stmartins.com

Photography by Megan Von Schönhoff and Tom Krawczyk

The Library of Congress Cataloging-in-Publication Data is available upon request.

ISBN 978-1-250-14632-8 (trade paperback)
ISBN 978-1-250-14631-1 (ebook)

Our books may be purchased in bulk for promotional, educational, or business
use. Please contact your local bookseller or the Macmillan Corporate and
Premium Sales Department at (800) 221-7945, extension 5442, or by email at
MacmillanSpecialMarkets@macmillan.com.

First Edition: January 2018

10 9 8 7 6 5 4 3 2 1

To Adriana, my best friend.

Many of our nostalgic moments revolve around food.

From cocktails to Jell-O, what amazing memories we have.

Thank you for being my sister.

Contents

4
Sides

5
Dinner

6
Dessert

7
Drinks

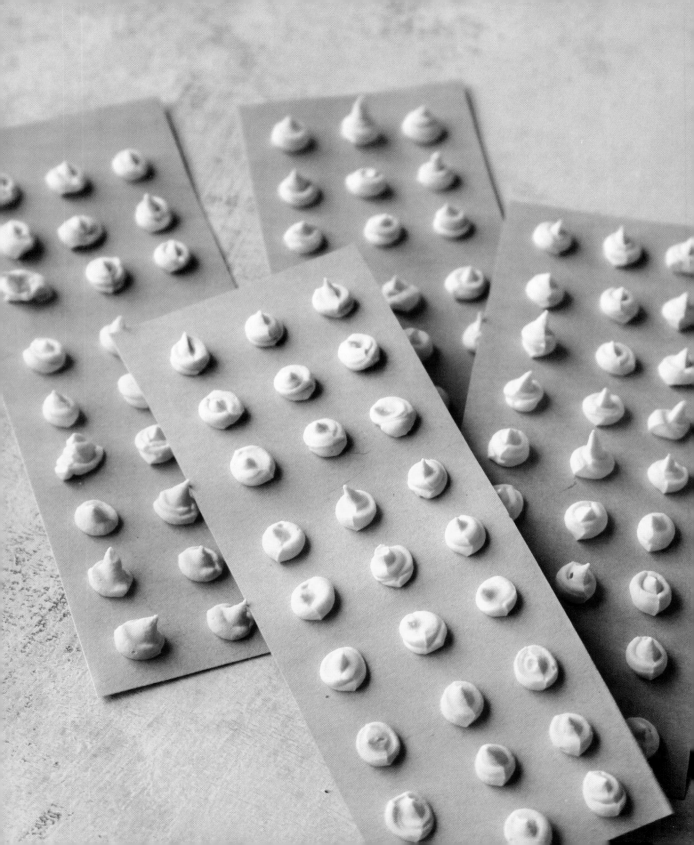

Introduction

The 1950s and 1960s are my two favorite culinary eras. With French influence from a role model of mine, Julia Child, and stately influence from another role model, Jacqueline Kennedy, parties were a bit more glamorous, and suburban high life included backyard barbecues, fondue nights, and cocktail parties. The drinks of the day included Vodka Gimlet Cocktails (page 215), and people gathered to gossip over a Cheesy Fondue (page 38). Families sat down to home-cooked meals, consisting of anything from No-Peek Chicken & Wild Rice Casserole (page 111) to Homemade Sloppy Joes (page 132). Dinner parties were a place to conduct business, impressing clients and the boss over Beef Wellington (page 148) and Grasshopper Pie (page 171). And traveling on vacation meant staying at a hotel and enjoying a Waldorf Salad (page 63).

We're in the revival era of midcentury entertainment with long-gone TV and movie franchises etching their mark on modern-day media. Shows like *Mad Men* have had many of us hooked. Baby names of eras past have surged in popularity. Reycling the best concepts from the past becomes a way to connect with others in the present—especially around food. (I particularly love the abundance of cheese found in many old-school appetizers!) You'll find common ground in shared experiences, between reminiscing over Grandma's version of Old-Fashioned Tuna Noodle Casserole (page 140) or laughing with your kids while making Old Time Popcorn Balls (page 192) just like you made growing up. And while there's a nostalgic elegance to recipes from the '50s and '60s, they still fit right at home in today's cooking. I love to make Egg-in-a-Hole (page 10) on Saturday mornings while I snuggle on the couch, binge-watching reruns of *Leave It to Beaver* and *I Love Lucy*. My Southern Deviled Eggs (page 42) are greedily snatched up when I invite friends over for a dinner party.

Cooking food from the past allows you to escape into a time-travel portal. For an hour, you don't need to update your phone or check up on your social media accounts. No matter how your family's schedules intersect, you can all find comfort in Reliable Chicken and Dumplings (page 131) and delight at Easy Strawberry Shortcake (page 199). The past brings people together, and when you can share a memory about a beloved dish, you spark deeper connections, turning mealtimes into the best parts of the day.

I hope this book inspires you to seek out those connections. Call up your siblings and see if they remember your grandparents' version of Classic Meat Loaf (page 112). Create memories of your own by making Homemade Chocolate Fudge Candies (page 168). It's your opportunity to laugh, reminisce, and turn what's old into something new by following in the footsteps of cooks from decades past. Why 103? When you come to our house, we want you to know you can always bring a friend, or two, or three. And when looking back on the best from the past, there's always time for a few more recipes.

—Addie Gundry

1

Breakfast

My husband and I savor our weekends, when we can enjoy a cup of freshly brewed coffee alongside a homemade breakfast. Whether we try to outdo each other with how many Fluffy Banana Pancakes (page 9) we can stack or enjoy a fancier meal of Three-Cheese Soufflés (page 21) while reading the morning paper, we can always count on breakfast to be the perfect start to the day.

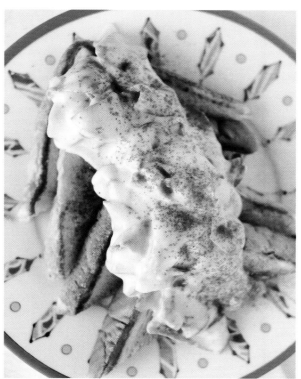

Vintage Coffee Cake

Yield: Serves 8 to 10 | Prep Time: 15 minutes | Cook Time: 45-55 minutes

In 1949, Duncan Hines, previously known for his restaurant recommendations, agreed to have his name used as a brand. His discriminating taste made him an authority on good cooking. When his line of cake mixes came out, he decided to use fresh eggs with his mixes instead of dehydrated ones because he thought they tasted better, and other cake-mix companies followed suit. This version follows in those footsteps.

INGREDIENTS

Cake

1 (15.25-ounce) box yellow cake mix

1 cup sour cream

⅓ cup vegetable or canola oil

4 large eggs

½ cup packed light brown sugar

1 teaspoon ground cinnamon

Glaze

¾ cup confectioners' sugar

1 teaspoon vanilla extract

2 tablespoons heavy cream

DIRECTIONS

1. *For the cake*: Preheat the oven to 325°F. Coat a 9 × 13-inch baking dish with cooking spray.

2. In a large bowl, combine the cake mix, sour cream, ¼ cup of water, vegetable oil, and eggs. Mix well.

3. In a small bowl, combine the brown sugar and cinnamon.

4. Layer half the cake batter in the prepared baking dish, then half the brown sugar mixture.

5. Top with the remaining batter, then the remaining brown sugar mixture.

6. Bake for 45 to 55 minutes, until the cake is set. Let cool in the baking dish while you prepare the glaze.

7. *For the glaze*: In a small bowl, combine the confectioners' sugar, vanilla, and heavy cream until it is smooth and has a pourable consistency.

8. Once the cake has cooled, drizzle the glaze over the cake. Cut into squares and serve.

New England Potato Doughnuts

Yield: 14–16 doughnuts | Prep Time: 20 minutes | Cook Time: 2-4 minutes per doughnut

Doughnuts may indeed be my favorite food, acceptable in the morning for breakfast and late at night for dessert. The first recipe for potato doughnuts was published in 1938 by Glenna Snow in the *Akron Beacon Journal*. Her recipe inspired the launch of a doughnut chain called Spudnut Shops that opened nationwide in the 1950s and is still around today.

INGREDIENTS

3 tablespoons unsalted butter, softened

¾ cup granulated sugar

1 large egg, at room temperature

1½ teaspoons vanilla extract

1 cup mashed cooked Yukon Gold potatoes

¼ cup buttermilk, at room temperature

1½ cups all-purpose flour, plus more for dusting

½ cup cake flour

1 teaspoon baking powder

1 teaspoon baking soda

½ teaspoon kosher salt

½ teaspoon grated nutmeg

Vegetable oil, for frying

Cinnamon sugar, for coating

DIRECTIONS

1. In the bowl of a stand mixer fitted with the paddle attachment, beat together the butter and granulated sugar on medium speed for 1 minute, until fluffy.

2. Add the egg and vanilla and mix until pale yellow.

3. Add the mashed potatoes and buttermilk and beat until smooth.

4. Add the all-purpose flour, cake flour, baking powder, baking soda, salt, and nutmeg. Mix until combined. The dough will be sticky.

5. Dust a work surface with flour. Place the dough on the counter and work a little bit of flour into the dough to make it easier to work with.

6. Gently press the dough down with your hands to about ½ inch thick.

7. Using a doughnut cutter or two biscuit cutters (one large and one small), cut into rounds. Reroll scraps to use all the dough.

8. In a large pot or Dutch oven, heat 2½ inches of vegetable oil to 375°F. Line a baking sheet with paper towels.

9. Carefully place a few doughnuts at a time in the hot oil and cook for 2 to 4 minutes on each side, until puffy and golden.

10. Transfer the cooked doughnuts to the prepared baking sheet. Let them cool for a few minutes, then toss in cinnamon sugar. Serve.

Fluffy Banana Pancakes

Yield: 12 pancakes | Prep Time: 15 minutes | Cook Time: 15 minutes

I used to stack piles of pancakes on my plate and see how many layers I could realistically fit on my fork. With pancakes this fluffy, I'd be shocked if you could cram on more than four, but I dare you to try! I even make this rich, sweet banana topping when I'm serving up regular pancakes or waffles.

INGREDIENTS

Banana Pancakes

2 cups buttermilk

1 cup mashed banana
(1–2 bananas)

2 large eggs

3 tablespoons unsalted butter, melted and cooled

2 teaspoons vanilla extract

2½ cups all-purpose flour

¼ cup granulated sugar

1 tablespoon baking powder

½ teaspoon baking soda

½ teaspoon kosher salt

½ cup finely chopped pecans

1 tablespoon unsalted butter

Toppings

1 tablespoon unsalted butter

2 bananas, sliced

1 tablespoon dark brown sugar

Toasted pecans, chopped

Maple syrup, warmed

DIRECTIONS

1. *For the banana pancakes:* Place the buttermilk in a large bowl. Whisk in the mashed banana, eggs, melted butter, and vanilla.

2. In a medium bowl, combine the flour, granulated sugar, baking powder, baking soda, salt, and chopped pecans.

3. Pour the flour mixture into the banana mixture and stir just until combined. Do not overmix.

4. Let the batter rest for 5 to 10 minutes.

5. In a large nonstick skillet, melt the butter over medium heat.

6. Pour about ⅓ cup of the batter into the skillet for each pancake. When small bubbles start to form on the pancakes, flip and cook on the other side until golden. Transfer the cooked pancakes to a plate and repeat with the remaining batter.

7. *For the toppings:* In a small skillet, melt the butter. Add the sliced bananas, sprinkle with the brown sugar, and cook until the bananas start to caramelize, about 5 minutes.

8. Top the pancakes with the caramelized bananas and toasted chopped pecans. Serve with warm maple syrup.

NOTE

To toast the pecans, cook them in a 350°F oven for 5 minutes.

Egg-in-a-Hole

Yield: Serves 1 | Prep Time: 5 minutes | Cook Time: 5 minutes

This vintage brunch recipe goes by many names: egg-in-a-hole, egg in a frame, gashouse egg, the Popeye, you name it. Popularized on 1950s diner menus across the country, this throwback recipe became a down-home staple that you can easily make at home today.

INGREDIENTS

1 thick slice of bread

1 tablespoon unsalted butter

1 large egg

Kosher salt and freshly ground black pepper

DIRECTIONS

1. Using a biscuit cutter or can, cut a hole in the center of the bread and set aside.

2. In a cast-iron or nonstick skillet, melt the butter over medium-low heat.

3. When the butter has melted, place the bread in the skillet with the smaller bread circle next to it.

4. Crack the egg directly in the hole of the bread.

5. Cook for 30 seconds or a bit longer before flipping over.

6. Sprinkle with salt and pepper, then flip and salt and pepper again. Turn the bread circle to brown the second side as well.

7. Cook until the bread is golden and the egg yolk starts to set up but is still soft. Try not to break the yolk.

8. Carefully transfer to a plate and serve with the cut-out piece of bread to dip into the yolk.

Berry Almond Scones

Yield: Serves 8 | Prep Time: 20 minutes | Cook Time: 18-22 minutes

My grandmother baked everything from scratch. She knew instantly whether someone had taken a shortcut or whether they "did the proper work," as she liked to say. One time, I made her these from-scratch scones, and after seeing her nod of satisfaction, I knew she approved.

INGREDIENTS

½ cup heavy cream

½ cup sour cream

1 teaspoon vanilla extract

2 cups all-purpose flour, plus more for dusting

½ cup plus 1 tablespoon sugar

2 teaspoons baking powder

¼ teaspoon baking soda

½ teaspoon kosher salt

1 teaspoon grated orange zest

¼ cup sliced almonds

½ cup (1 stick) unsalted butter, cold, cut into small cubes, plus 1 tablespoon unsalted butter, melted

1 cup fresh or frozen mixed berries, thawed if frozen

DIRECTIONS

1. Preheat the oven to 425°F. Line a baking sheet with parchment paper.

2. In a small bowl, mix the heavy cream, sour cream, and vanilla.

3. In a large bowl, whisk together the flour, ½ cup of the sugar, the baking powder, baking soda, salt, orange zest, and almonds. Add the cubed butter to the flour mixture and toss to coat.

4. Add the cream mixture to the flour mixture and mix until combined.

5. Dust a work surface with flour. Place the dough on the work surface and knead six to eight times.

6. Roll the dough out to a 12-inch square.

7. Take the top and bottom of the dough and fold toward the center into three equal layers, like a letter. Then take the left and right sides of the dough and fold toward the center into three equal layers, like a letter. You'll end up with a 4-inch square. Chill for 10 minutes.

8. On a floured surface, roll out the chilled dough into a 12-inch square.

9. Sprinkle the berries over the dough and gently press them down.

10. Fold the edges over to create a circle 7 to 8 inches in diameter. The berries will now be covered by the dough.

11. Cut the dough into 8 wedges. Place the scones on the baking sheet.

12. Brush melted butter over each scone and sprinkle each with the remaining 1 tablespoon sugar.

13. Bake for 18 to 22 minutes, or until the scones are golden. Transfer to a wire rack to cool slightly. Serve warm.

Biscuits and Gravy

Yield: Serves 8 | Prep Time: 15 minutes | Cook Time: 20-25 minutes

Whenever we went on a family road trip, my dad bragged about this breakfast place where his family used to stop when he traveled to visit family in Texas, which served up the best biscuits and gravy he'd ever eaten. Our family was always on a quest to find something just as good, and it wasn't until this homemade version that I finally found it.

INGREDIENTS

1 pound breakfast sausage

⅓ cup all-purpose flour

2 cups whole milk

2 cups half-and-half

½ teaspoon kosher salt

1 teaspoon freshly ground black pepper

⅛–¼ teaspoon cayenne pepper

8 biscuits, homemade or from a can (baked according to package instructions)

DIRECTIONS

1. In a large skillet, crumble and brown the sausage over medium-high heat until fully cooked.

2. Reduce the heat to medium. Sprinkle half the flour over the sausage and stir until the flour is fully mixed in. Add the rest of the flour and cook, stirring, for another minute.

3. Turn the heat up to medium-high and stir in the milk and half-and-half.

4. Add the salt, black pepper, and cayenne pepper.

5. Stir the mixture until a thick gravy forms, about 5 minutes. Add a bit more milk or half-and-half if needed.

6. Serve the gravy over warm biscuits.

Hot Cross Buns

Yield: 15 buns | Prep Time: 45 minutes plus proofing time | Cook Time: 20-25 minutes

Hot Cross Buns were a staple for my mom. The family-owned corner bakery was run by a gregarious baker who would sneak in an extra bun when my mom got a few for the family.

INGREDIENTS

Buns

1½ cups whole milk, lukewarm

½ cup granulated sugar

1 tablespoon active dry yeast

4–4½ cups all-purpose flour

½ teaspoon kosher salt

½ teaspoon ground cinnamon

½ teaspoon grated nutmeg

½ teaspoon ground cardamom

2 large eggs, at room temperature, beaten

4 tablespoons (½ stick) unsalted butter, softened

1 cup dried mixed fruits

2 teaspoons grated orange zest

1 tablespoon vegetable oil

Syrup

¼ cup granulated sugar

Icing

½ cup confectioners' sugar

2 tablespoons cream cheese, at room temperature

1 tablespoon unsalted butter, softened

1 teaspoon vanilla extract

1½ teaspoons water

DIRECTIONS

1. *For the buns:* In a small bowl, combine the milk, granulated sugar, and yeast. Stir until combined and let rest for 15 minutes.

2. In the bowl of a stand mixer fitted with the paddle attachment, mix together 4 cups of the flour, the salt, cinnamon, nutmeg, and cardamom until combined. Mix in the eggs and butter.

3. Pour the yeast mixture over the flour. Switch to the dough hook attachment and mix for 5 to 6 minutes. Add the dried fruit and orange zest and mix for another minute. Add more flour if the dough is wet. It should be soft and elastic.

4. Coat a large bowl with the vegetable oil, place the dough in the bowl, and roll it so all sides are coated with a bit of oil. Cover with plastic wrap and place in a warm spot until doubled in size, 1 to 2 hours.

5. Preheat the oven to 375°F. Line a baking sheet with parchment paper.

6. Divide the dough into 15 pieces. Roll each piece of dough into a bun and place on the prepared baking sheet. Cover with a damp tea towel and set aside for 30 minutes, until the buns have doubled. Bake the buns for 20 to 25 minutes, until golden brown.

7. *For the syrup:* In a small saucepan, combine a ¼ cup of water and the granulated sugar and bring to a boil over low heat. Let it boil for a few minutes until the syrup has thickened. Remove from the heat and brush the tops with the syrup.

8. *For the icing:* In a small bowl, whisk together the confectioners' sugar, cream cheese, butter, vanilla, and water until a creamy consistency is achieved. Transfer the icing to a piping bag and pipe an "X" over each bun. Serve.

Bacon and Gruyère Quiche

Yield: Serves 8 | Prep Time: 20 minutes | Cook Time: 40-45 minutes

Quiche was popularized in the United States in the 1950s, and given its heartiness and portability, it's easy to see why. Take it to a luncheon or brunch potluck with friends; it's one dish that never goes out of style.

INGREDIENTS

12 ounces bacon

2 teaspoons olive oil

3 large shallots, sliced

4 fresh thyme sprigs

6 large eggs

1½ cups heavy cream

1 (9-inch) deep-dish pie crust (store-bought or homemade)

1 cup shredded Gruyère cheese

Pinch of grated nutmeg

Pinch of cayenne pepper

DIRECTIONS

1. Preheat the oven to 375°F.

2. Cut the bacon into small pieces and cook until crisp. Drain on paper towels.

3. In a medium pan, heat the olive oil over medium heat. Add the shallots and 3 of the thyme sprigs and cook, stirring, until the shallots are soft and starting to caramelize. Turn off the heat and set aside; remove and discard the thyme.

4. In a large bowl, whisk together the eggs and heavy cream. Set aside.

5. Spread the shallots over the bottom of the pie shell.

6. Add half the bacon and half the Gruyère over the shallots.

7. Pour the egg mixture over the bacon and cheese. Sprinkle with the nutmeg and cayenne.

8. Bake for 20 minutes.

9. Spread the remaining bacon and Gruyère over the top of the quiche.

10. Bake for 20 to 25 minutes more, until the quiche is set and golden.

11. Let cool for 15 minutes before cutting. Garnish with a sprig of thyme, if desired, and serve.

Three-Cheese Soufflés

Yield: Serves 8 | Prep Time: 50 minutes | Cook Time: 40-45 minutes

While many Americans grew to love soufflés back in the '50s and '60s, my own love for the dish developed when I lived in France. I've made all sorts of soufflés, from savory to sweet, but this classic breakfast version might be my favorite of the bunch.

INGREDIENTS

⅓ cup unsalted butter, cut into cubes

⅓ cup all-purpose flour

2 cups whole milk

1 teaspoon dry mustard

¼ teaspoon kosher salt

¼ teaspoon freshly ground white pepper

2 pinches of grated nutmeg

1½ cups shredded Gruyère cheese

1 cup shredded cheddar cheese

¼ cup shredded Parmesan cheese

6 large eggs

½ teaspoon cream of tartar

DIRECTIONS

1. In a small saucepan, melt the butter over medium-high heat. Stir in the flour and mix until smooth, about 1 minute. Slowly whisk in the milk, mustard, salt, white pepper, and nutmeg.

2. Bring to a boil and cook, stirring continuously, for 1 to 2 minutes, or until thickened. Reduce the heat to medium, add the Gruyère, cheddar, and Parmesan, and stir until melted. Remove from the heat and transfer to a large bowl to cool.

3. Separate the eggs. Place the egg whites in a medium bowl and let sit for 30 minutes.

4. In a small bowl, beat the egg yolks until thick, about 4 minutes. Slowly stir in ⅓ cup of the hot cheese mixture to temper the eggs.

5. Add the tempered egg yolk mixture to the remaining cheese mixture and stir until combined. Let cool for 20 to 30 minutes.

6. Preheat the oven to 325°F. Place eight ungreased 8-ounce ramekins in 2 baking pans.

7. Beat the egg whites with the cream of tartar on high speed until stiff.

8. Using a spatula, stir about one-quarter of the egg whites into the cheese mixture. Carefully fold in the rest of the egg whites.

9. Spoon the mixture into the ramekins, filling them about three-quarters full. Pour 1 inch of hot water into the baking pan around the ramekins, being careful not to get water in the soufflés.

10. Bake for 40 minutes, or until the tops have puffed up and are golden.

11. Remove from the water and serve.

Creamed Chipped Beef

Yield: Serves 4 | Prep Time: 5 minutes | Cook Time: 15 minutes

Chipped beef was a standard breakfast option served to members of the United States Navy during the mid-twentieth century. It was easy enough to make in bulk, relatively inexpensive, and served the purpose of filling up the sailors before they headed out for the day.

INGREDIENTS

2 (2.25-ounce) jars sliced dried beef, cut into ½-inch strips

3 tablespoons unsalted butter

¼ cup finely diced onion

3 tablespoons all-purpose flour

½ teaspoon kosher salt

¼ teaspoon freshly ground black pepper

⅛ teaspoon cayenne pepper

¼ teaspoon dry mustard

1 cup whole milk

1 cup half-and-half

1 tablespoon Worcestershire sauce

4 thick slices white bread, toasted and cut in half

Smoked paprika (optional)

DIRECTIONS

1. In a medium bowl, cover the beef strips with warm water. Let soak for 2 minutes and drain.

2. In a large skillet, melt the butter over medium heat. Add the onion and cook, stirring, for 3 to 4 minutes, until soft.

3. Stir in the flour, salt, black pepper, cayenne, and mustard. Cook for 1 minute.

4. Add the milk, half-and-half, and Worcestershire sauce. Mix well.

5. Bring to a boil, reduce the heat to low, and stir in the beef.

6. Cook, stirring continuously, for 3 to 4 minutes, until the sauce has thickened.

7. Place the toast slices on a plate and spoon an equal amount of the beef mixture over each toast.

8. Sprinkle with a small amount of smoked paprika, if desired, and serve.

Old-Fashioned Doughnut Muffins

Yield: 24 mini muffins | Prep Time: 20 minutes | Cook Time: 10-11 minutes

This recipe mashup boasts the soft texture of a doughnut in the cute, portable shape of a muffin, and I can't get enough of them. Doughnuts nowadays are an over-the-top indulgence, lathered in layers of gooey frosting and glaze. This is the kind of miniature doughnut treat I go for when I'm craving something sweet but manageable.

INGREDIENTS

1 large egg

5 tablespoons unsalted butter, softened, plus 4 tablespoons (½ stick) unsalted butter, melted

¾ cup granulated sugar

¼ cup packed light brown sugar

1 teaspoon vanilla extract

½ teaspoon almond extract

¾ cup buttermilk

1¼ cups all-purpose flour

1½ teaspoons baking powder

4 teaspoons ground cinnamon

1 teaspoon grated nutmeg

¼ teaspoon kosher salt

DIRECTIONS

1. Preheat the oven to 350°F. Coat a 24-well mini-muffin pan with cooking spray.

2. In the bowl of a stand mixer fitted with the paddle attachment, combine the egg, softened butter, ¼ cup of the granulated sugar, the brown sugar, vanilla, and almond extract and beat on medium-high until light and fluffy, 3 to 4 minutes.

3. Add the buttermilk and mix until combined.

4. Add the flour, baking powder, 2 teaspoons of the cinnamon, the nutmeg, and the salt. Beat on low just until combined.

5. Using a small ice cream scoop (about 2 tablespoons), drop batter into each muffin cup.

6. Bake for 10 to 11 minutes, until the muffins are set. Test using a cake tester or wooden toothpick.

7. Set the muffin tin on a wire rack to cool for 10 minutes.

8. Place the melted butter in a small bowl. Combine the remaining ½ cup sugar and 2 teaspoons cinnamon in another medium bowl.

9. Remove the muffins from the pan, brush the melted butter on the top and sides of each muffin, then roll in the cinnamon sugar to coat. Serve.

2

Appetizers

Retro cocktail parties and neighborhood backyard parties are so much fun! In the middle of the century, they were a key element of socializing, with hosting skills on display front and center. Finger foods and cocktails were presented with immaculate care among fresh flowers and other décor, and the best parties would get raves for weeks. More intimate social engagements with just a couple of guests allowed hosts to dabble with new recipes without the pressure of appeasing an intimidating crowd. These appetizers will help you re-create the magic of the '50s and '60s the next time you're expecting company.

Party Cheese Ball

Yield: Serves 8 to 10 | Prep Time: 10 minutes | Chill Time: Overnight

The first time a recipe for a cheese ball appeared in print was in *Food of My Friends*, a cookbook published in 1944 by *Minneapolis Star-Journal* columnist Virginia Safford. Soon after, everyone seemed to have their own variation on the classic party favorite, and it became a staple of 1950s house parties.

INGREDIENTS

3 cups grated extra-sharp cheddar cheese, room temperature

½ (8-ounce) package cream cheese, room temperature

4 ounces goat cheese, room temperature

2 tablespoons mayonnaise

1 teaspoon Dijon mustard

2 green onions, finely minced

1 tablespoon Worcestershire sauce

¼ teaspoon freshly ground black pepper

1 tablespoon brandy

1½ cups chopped pecans

Crackers, for serving

DIRECTIONS

1. Line a medium bowl with plastic wrap.

2. In another medium bowl, combine the cheddar cheese, cream cheese, goat cheese, mayonnaise, mustard, green onions, Worcestershire sauce, pepper, and brandy. Mix well until all the ingredients are incorporated. Shape the mixture into a ball and place in the plastic wrap–lined bowl. Cover.

3. Chill for several hours or overnight.

4. Roll the cheese ball in the chopped pecans.

5. Serve with crackers.

Super-Easy Crab Puffs

Yield: 16 puffs | Prep Time: 30 minutes | Cook Time: 20 minutes

This seems like the kind of appetizer *Mad Men*'s Betty Draper would serve at one of her 1950s dinner parties while sipping a Vodka Gimlet Cocktail (page 215). These bite-size snacks are ideal for munching on while milling about and hearing the latest gossip from your friends and family.

INGREDIENTS

¾ (8-ounce) package cream cheese, at room temperature

1 tablespoon sour cream

12 ounces canned crabmeat, drained

2 green onions: 1 minced, 1 chopped

1 garlic clove, minced

½ teaspoon lemon zest

2 teaspoons fresh lemon juice

½ teaspoon Worcestershire sauce

Kosher salt and freshly ground black pepper

All-purpose flour, for dusting

1 sheet frozen puff pastry, thawed

1 large egg, beaten with 1 tablespoon water

DIRECTIONS

1. Preheat the oven to 400°F. Line a baking sheet with parchment paper.

2. In a medium bowl, combine the cream cheese, sour cream, crabmeat, minced green onion, garlic, lemon zest, lemon juice, Worcestershire sauce, and salt and pepper to taste. Mix well.

3. Lightly flour a work surface. Roll out the pastry to about a 12-inch square. Cut into 16 squares.

4. Fill each square with about 2 tablespoons of the crab filling.

5. Fold the dough over on each side of the square to create a raised, open cup.

6. Brush each pastry with the egg. Place on the prepared baking sheet.

7. Bake for 20 minutes until puffed and golden.

8. Sprinkle with the chopped green onion. Serve.

Shrimp Cocktail

Yield: Serves 4 to 6 | Prep Time: 5 minutes | Cook Time: 20 minutes

Shrimp cocktails give off an air of class and sophistication despite being so easy. It's a "pinkies up" kind of food. Shrimp cocktails made regular appearances at the fanciest dinner parties in the '50s and '60s and were even a mainstay in the flashy, high-stakes casino world. I prefer to make the cocktail sauce from scratch so I can control how spicy it is.

INGREDIENTS

Shrimp

5 sprigs fresh thyme

2 sprigs fresh parsley

2 bay leaves

1 onion, quartered

1 tablespoon kosher salt

1 teaspoon whole black peppercorns

1 cup white wine

1 lemon

1 tablespoon Tabasco Chipotle sauce

1 pound deveined shell-on jumbo shrimp

Cocktail Sauce

½ cup chili sauce

2 tablespoons prepared horseradish

½ teaspoon fresh lemon juice

½ teaspoon Worcestershire sauce

½ teaspoon Tabasco Chipotle sauce

¼ teaspoon kosher salt

1 lemon, sliced, for serving

DIRECTIONS

1. *For the shrimp:* In a large pot, combine the thyme, parsley, bay leaves, onion, salt, peppercorns, wine, and 2 cups water.

2. Cut the lemon in half and squeeze the juice from each half into the pot. Throw the lemon halves into the pot as well.

3. Bring the mixture to a boil over medium heat.

4. Turn off the heat and let sit for 10 minutes to infuse the mixture. Fill a large bowl with ice and water and set it nearby.

5. Remove the lemon halves and add the Tabasco and the shrimp.

6. Simmer the shrimp over medium heat for 5 to 8 minutes.

7. Remove the shrimp and place in the ice bath to stop the cooking.

8. Drain and peel the shrimp. Place on a platter.

9. *For the cocktail sauce:* In a medium bowl, combine the chili sauce, horseradish, lemon juice, Worcestershire sauce, Tabasco, and salt.

10. Serve the chilled shrimp with the sauce and lemon slices.

Pigs in a Blanket

Yield: 24 pieces | Prep Time: 20 minutes | Cook Time: 20 minutes

It used to be that a cocktail party wasn't quite complete without a tray of pigs in a blanket at the ready. My parents carried on that tradition into my childhood. Popular in Dutch communities in the twentieth century, this dish made its way into America's increasingly diverse cuisine.

INGREDIENTS

All-purpose flour, for dusting

1 sheet frozen puff pastry, thawed

2 tablespoons Dijon mustard

⅓ cup shredded cheddar cheese

1 large egg, beaten with 1 tablespoon water

32 mini hot dogs

Poppy seeds

DIRECTIONS

1. Preheat the oven to 425°F. Line a baking sheet with parchment paper.

2. Dust a work surface with flour. Place the pastry on the work surface and roll it out into a 13-inch square.

3. Spread the mustard evenly over the pastry, then sprinkle the cheddar cheese over the top.

4. Cut 8 strips from the square, then cut across 3 times to make 24 strips.

5. Brush the edges of the dough with the egg.

6. Roll each mini hot dog in one strip of dough. Place on the prepared baking sheet seam-side down.

7. Brush the top of each with the egg and sprinkle on some poppy seeds.

8. Bake for 20 minutes, until the pastry is puffy and golden brown. Serve.

Oysters Rockefeller

Yield: Serves 8 | Prep Time: 10 minutes | Cook Time: 5 minutes

Add just the right combination of spices to fresh oysters, and you've got a five-star dish that epitomizes the height of luxury. Plus, the Pernod, an anise-flavored liqueur, can be used again to make other specialty drinks. It doesn't get much better than that!

INGREDIENTS

1 garlic clove

1 small shallot

2 cups fresh spinach

1 bunch fresh watercress, stems trimmed

½ cup sliced green onions

¾ cup (1½ sticks) unsalted butter, softened

½ cup dried bread crumbs or panko bread crumbs

2 tablespoons Pernod

1 teaspoon fennel seeds, ground

1 teaspoon hot pepper sauce

1 pound rock salt (use kosher salt if you can't find rock salt)

24 fresh oysters, shucked, shells reserved

¼ cup grated Parmesan cheese

DIRECTIONS

1. Preheat the oven to broil.

2. In a food processor, combine the garlic, shallot, spinach, watercress, and green onions. Pulse until chopped.

3. Add the butter, bread crumbs, Pernod, fennel seeds, and hot pepper sauce and pulse again to combine.

4. Sprinkle the rock salt in a ¼-inch-thick layer in a 9 × 13-inch baking dish.

5. Place the oysters in the half shells on top of the salt.

6. Top each oyster with 1 tablespoon of the spinach mixture and sprinkle with Parmesan.

7. Place the baking dish on the middle rack of the oven and broil for 5 minutes, until the spinach mixture is bubbling and golden. Let cool for 5 minutes before serving.

Cheesy Fondue

Yield: Serves 4 | Prep Time: 15 minutes | Cook Time: 15 minutes

During the 1950s and '60s, fondue parties were all the rage, with stainless-steel pots in Scandinavian designs becoming particularly fashionable. The designs of the pots themselves became somewhat of a talking piece, with artists like Peter Max creating patterned designs that would impress guests. In the late '60s and early '70s, fondue pots became a popular gift for weddings to keep the fondue party rolling.

INGREDIENTS

8 ounces Gruyère cheese, grated

8 ounces Emmental cheese, grated

2 tablespoons cornstarch

1 cup dry white wine

1 garlic clove, minced

1 tablespoon fresh lemon juice

1 tablespoon kirsch or brandy

½ teaspoon dry mustard

⅛ teaspoon grated nutmeg

For Dipping

Small skin-on roasted fingerling potatoes

Assorted lightly steamed vegetables

Sliced apples and pears

Cubed French or sourdough bread

DIRECTIONS

1. In a large bowl, combine the Gruyère and Emmental cheeses with the cornstarch and toss well.

2. In a fondue pot or large heavy saucepan, bring the wine, garlic, and lemon juice to a simmer over medium heat.

3. Add the cheese mixture into the liquid a little at a time. Stir after each addition.

4. Once the mixture is smooth, add in the kirsch, mustard, and nutmeg.

5. Serve hot and bubbling with assorted dippers.

Cream Cheese–Stuffed Celery

Yield: Serves 24 │ Prep Time: 10 minutes │ Cook Time: N/A

Stuffed celery became a natural hit at dinner parties and luncheons in the 1960s since the groove in the center practically begged to be filled. There were different variations on stuffed celery to fit the occasion: soft cheeses topped with spices like paprika for sophisticated events or nuts and cranberries for holidays. I prefer this cream cheese variation since it can be dressed up or down for any setting.

INGREDIENTS

1 (8-ounce) package cream cheese, at room temperature

6 tablespoons chopped pimento-stuffed olives

A few pinches of freshly ground black pepper

1 large bunch celery, cut into 3- to 4-inch-long pieces

DIRECTIONS

1. In a medium bowl, mix the cream cheese, chopped olives, and pepper until creamy.

2. Fill the cavities of the celery with the cream cheese mixture. Serve.

Southern Deviled Eggs

Yield: Serves 12 | Prep Time: 20 minutes | Cook Time: N/A

You're sure to channel your inner June Cleaver when you whip up these crowd-pleasing deviled eggs. I've added a slight Southern twist in the form of sweet pickle relish to give the dish an even more striking flavor, but feel free to omit it if you wish.

INGREDIENTS

6 large hard-boiled eggs, peeled

2 tablespoons mayonnaise

2 tablespoons sour cream

1 teaspoon apple cider vinegar

½ teaspoon dry mustard

1½ tablespoons sweet pickle relish (optional)

¼ teaspoon kosher salt

¼ teaspoon freshly ground black pepper

Pimento slices, cut in half

Baby dill pickles, sliced

Paprika

DIRECTIONS

1. Halve the hard-boiled eggs lengthwise. Scoop the yolks into a medium bowl and set the whites aside.

2. Mash the yolks with a fork.

3. Add the mayonnaise, sour cream, vinegar, mustard, relish (if using), salt, and pepper and mix until smooth.

4. Set the egg whites on a serving platter, rounded-side down. Using a piping bag or a spoon, fill the cavity of each egg white with the egg yolk filling.

5. Top each egg half with a pimento slice and a dill pickle slice. Sprinkle with paprika and serve.

Rumaki

Yield: 8 pieces | Prep Time: 10 minutes plus 30 minutes marinating time | Cook Time: 6 minutes

Rumaki is a Polynesian appetizer that you'll want to break out if you're trying to impress your family and friends. It was first popularized in the 1940s in tiki restaurants in San Francisco and Los Angeles, but soon made its way into dinner parties across the country.

INGREDIENTS

2 tablespoons teriyaki sauce

1 teaspoon finely grated peeled fresh ginger

1 tablespoon light brown sugar

4 chicken livers, cut in half

8 water chestnuts, drained

4 bacon slices, cut in half

DIRECTIONS

1. In a small bowl, combine the teriyaki sauce, ginger, and brown sugar.

2. Add the chicken livers and water chestnuts and toss to coat.

3. Cover and marinate in the refrigerator for 30 minutes.

4. Preheat the oven to broil. Line a baking sheet with parchment paper.

5. Remove the livers and chestnuts from the marinade.

6. Place 1 piece of bacon on the prepared baking sheet, then layer 1 piece of liver followed by 1 water chestnut on top. Wrap the bacon around the liver and water chestnut and secure with a toothpick. Repeat with the remaining bacon, livers, and water chestnuts.

7. Broil the rumaki about 2 inches from the heat for 6 minutes, until the bacon is crisp and the liver is slightly pink. Serve.

Slow Cooker Party Meatballs in Grape Jelly

Yield: 48-50 meatballs | Prep Time: 5 minutes | Cook Time: 3-4 hours on High or 8 hours on Low

Slow cookers first started to appear on store shelves in the late 1960s, and it wasn't long before they made their way into homes across America. When they first appeared on the scene, they opened up so many options for home cooks, including allowing party hosts the chance to serve up their favorite party meatballs while keeping them toasty warm all evening long.

INGREDIENTS

1 (24-ounce) bottle barbecue sauce

1½ cups grape jelly

2 tablespoons Worcestershire sauce

3 pounds frozen meatballs

DIRECTIONS

1. Lightly coat the insert of a 6-quart slow cooker with cooking spray.

2. Add the barbecue sauce, grape jelly, and Worcestershire sauce and mix well.

3. Add the meatballs and stir to coat completely.

4. Cover and cook for 3 to 4 hours on High or 8 hours on Low. Spoon onto a serving platter, stick a toothpick in each meatball, and serve.

3

Soups, Salads, and Sandwiches

The range of flavors found in the dishes in this chapter makes me regret all those days when I'd pack some boring frozen meal for lunch. Just wait until you try the candied pecans in the Waldorf Salad (page 63) or seek out the smoky bacon bits in the Chicken Corn Chowder (page 51). And the gooey, melted cheese on the Monte Cristo (page 75) has me aching to make it again the next day.

Chicken Corn Chowder

Yield: Serves 6 or 7 | Prep Time: 15 minutes | Cook Time: 30 minutes

Different variations on corn chowder played off ingredients that companies were trying to sell, from frozen corn to flour to sweetened condensed milk, that made it a popular recipe found in print advertisements. Chowders were frequently made in New England homes though their popularity was felt nationwide.

INGREDIENTS

4 tablespoons (½ stick) unsalted butter, cubed

1 large red bell pepper, diced

1 onion, diced

4 garlic cloves, minced

⅓ cup all-purpose flour

5½ cups chicken broth

½ cup white wine

3 Yukon Gold potatoes, peeled and cut into ½-inch dice

1 tablespoon fresh thyme, minced

1 teaspoon kosher salt

½ teaspoon freshly ground black pepper

1 pound boneless, skinless chicken breasts, cooked and shredded

2½ cups fresh or frozen corn

1½ cups heavy cream

8 slices bacon, cooked and crumbled, for garnish

Sliced fresh chives, for garnish

DIRECTIONS

1. In a large pot, melt the butter over medium heat. Add the bell pepper and onion and cook until tender.

2. Add the garlic and cook for 30 seconds.

3. Whisk in the flour and cook for 2 minutes, being careful not to burn the flour.

4. While whisking, add the broth and wine and whisk until blended.

5. Add the potatoes, thyme, salt, and black pepper.

6. Bring to a boil, then reduce the heat to medium-low and cook for 10 minutes, or until the potatoes are fork-tender.

7. Add the chicken, corn, and heavy cream. Simmer for 10 to 15 minutes.

8. Serve topped with the crumbled bacon and chives.

NOTE

To cook the chicken, place 2 medium boneless, skinless chicken breasts on a baking sheet and bake at 350°F for 30 minutes.

Slow Cooker Split Pea Soup

Yield: Serves 6 to 8 | Prep Time: 20 minutes | Cook Time: 6-7 hours on High

I was never allowed to leave the dinner table until I had eaten most of the veggies on my plate—maybe you can relate. While there were some veggies that I dragged my feet on (hello, green beans!), I barely even noticed that recipes like my grandma's split pea soup were chock-full of them.

INGREDIENTS

1 (16-ounce) bag green split peas, rinsed and drained

1 cup finely chopped carrots

2 celery stalks, finely chopped

½ cup finely chopped onion

1 tablespoon minced garlic

⅓ cup chopped fresh parsley

1 tablespoon chopped fresh thyme

2 bay leaves

½ teaspoon kosher salt, plus more if needed

½ teaspoon freshly ground black pepper, plus more if needed

2 cups cubed smoked ham steak

5–6 cups chicken broth

DIRECTIONS

1. Lightly spray the insert of an 8-quart slow cooker with cooking spray.

2. Layer the split peas, carrots, celery, onion, garlic, parsley, thyme, bay leaves, salt, pepper, and ham steak in the slow cooker. Stir to mix.

3. Add 4 to 5 cups of the broth to cover the ingredients.

4. Cover and cook for 6 to 7 hours on High, until the peas are tender.

5. Remove and discard the bay leaves. Add more broth if needed and season with salt and pepper, if desired. Ladle into bowls and serve.

Slow Cooker Beef Stew

Yield: Serves 8 | Prep Time: 15 minutes | Cook Time: 4-5 hours on High or 8-10 hours on Low

Beef stew was a mainstay on dinner tables in the '50s. It had everything you could want out of a meal: plenty of vegetables, hearty meat, and the ability to be easily reheated. I love this slow cooker version because I can prep it in the morning and let it simmer all day while I'm at work or out running errands.

INGREDIENTS

2 pounds beef stew meat, cut into 1-inch pieces

1 teaspoon kosher salt

½ teaspoon freshly ground black pepper

4 tablespoons all-purpose flour

1 tablespoon olive oil

1 pound Yukon Gold potatoes, peeled and cut into 2-inch cubes

4 carrots, cut into 1-inch pieces

2 onions, cut into wedges

4 garlic cloves, minced

2½ cups beef broth

1 (6-ounce) can tomato paste

1 (14-ounce) can fire-roasted diced tomatoes

1 tablespoon Worcestershire sauce

1 teaspoon dried thyme

1 bay leaf

1 cup frozen peas

DIRECTIONS

1. Season the beef stew meat with the salt and pepper.

2. Coat the beef with 2 tablespoons of the flour.

3. In a large skillet, heat the olive oil over medium heat. Add the beef and cook until browned, about 3 minutes on each side.

4. Lightly spray the insert of an 8-quart slow cooker with cooking spray.

5. Put the potatoes, carrots, onions, and garlic in the slow cooker.

6. Top with the browned beef.

7. Add 2 cups of the broth, the tomato paste, diced tomatoes, Worcestershire sauce, thyme, and bay leaf. Stir to combine.

8. Cover and cook for 4 to 5 hours on High or for 8 to 10 hours on Low.

9. Remove and discard the bay leaf.

10. In a small bowl, combine the remaining 2 tablespoons flour and ½ cup broth and mix well. Stir the flour mixture and the peas into the beef stew.

11. Cook for 15 minutes more, until the mixture thickens. Ladle into bowls and serve.

Chicken and Sausage Gumbo

Yield: Serves 8 to 10 | Prep Time: 15 minutes | Cook Time: 50-65 minutes

Julia Child popularized the French dish bouillabaisse in the 1950s and '60s. It was only natural that the dish known as the New Orleans version of bouillabaisse would find its niche, too. I chose to keep the seafood to a minimum to make this dish accessible all year round.

INGREDIENTS

1 cup vegetable oil

1⅓ cups all-purpose flour

3 green bell peppers, diced

2 celery stalks, diced

1 small onion, diced

5 garlic cloves, minced

2 cups fresh or frozen chopped okra

1 pound andouille sausage, sliced

1 (14-ounce) can fire-roasted tomatoes

1 tablespoon Creole seasoning

2 teaspoons dried thyme

1–2 teaspoons cayenne pepper

1–2 teaspoons kosher salt

1–2 teaspoons freshly ground black pepper

6 cups chicken broth

2 tablespoons Worcestershire sauce

2 cups shredded cooked chicken (see Note)

½ pound shrimp, peeled and deveined

3 bay leaves

Cooked white rice, for serving

Hot sauce, for serving

DIRECTIONS

1. In a large Dutch oven, heat the vegetable oil over medium-high heat. Whisk in the flour. Cook, whisking and stirring continuously, for 15 to 20 minutes, until the roux takes on a dark brown color. Be careful not to burn the roux!

2. Add the bell peppers, celery, onion, garlic, and okra. Mix until combined. Cook, stirring every 10 to 15 seconds, until the vegetables start to soften, about 10 minutes.

3. Add the sausage, tomatoes, Creole seasoning, thyme, cayenne, salt, and black pepper. Cook, stirring occasionally, for 5 minutes more.

4. Gradually add the broth, Worcestershire sauce, shredded chicken, shrimp, and bay leaves.

5. Reduce the heat to medium-low and simmer for 10 to 15 minutes, until the shrimp are fully cooked and the vegetables are tender.

6. Taste and adjust the seasoning, if necessary. Remove the bay leaves.

7. Serve with rice and hot sauce.

NOTE

To cook the chicken, place 2 medium boneless, skinless chicken breasts on a baking sheet and bake at 350°F for 30 minutes. Remove from the oven and shred.

Chili con Carne

Yield: Serves 4 | Prep Time: 15 minutes | Cook Time: 1 hour 15 minutes

Family-run chili parlors were all the rage even before the 1950s and continued to make their mark throughout the mid-twentieth century across Texas and parts of the Midwest. You can re-create the magic of those chili parlors at home with this flavorful dish.

INGREDIENTS

1 tablespoon olive oil

3 garlic cloves, minced

1 onion, diced

1 red or green bell pepper, diced

1 pound ground beef

1½ teaspoons chili powder

2 teaspoon smoked paprika

1½ teaspoons ground cumin

¼ teaspoon cayenne pepper

1 teaspoon onion powder

½ teaspoon light brown sugar

¼ cup tomato paste

1 (14-ounce) can fire-roasted diced tomatoes

1 (14-ounce) can red kidney beans, drained

¾ cup beef broth

½ teaspoon kosher salt

¼ teaspoon freshly ground black pepper

Grated cheddar cheese and sour cream, for serving

DIRECTIONS

1. In a medium Dutch oven or saucepan, heat the olive oil over medium heat. Add the garlic and onion and cook for 1 to 2 minutes.

2. Add the bell pepper and cook for 2 minutes.

3. Raise the heat to high. Add the ground beef and cook, breaking it up as it cooks, until browned and almost cooked through, about 5 minutes.

4. Add the chili powder, paprika, cumin, cayenne, onion powder, and brown sugar. Cook, stirring occasionally, until the beef is fully cooked.

5. Stir in the tomato paste, tomatoes, kidney beans, ½ cup of the broth, the salt, and the black pepper.

6. Bring to a simmer. Cover and cook for 30 minutes. Add the remaining ¼ cup beef broth and cook for 30 minutes more.

7. Taste and adjust the seasoning, if needed.

8. Serve with grated cheddar cheese and sour cream.

Watergate Salad

Yield: Serves 6 to 8 | Prep Time: 5 minutes | Chill Time: 4 hours

This vintage recipe debuted in the early 1970s when Kraft Foods introduced its instant pistachio pudding mix. Originally called Pistachio Pineapple Delight, a Chicago newspaper dubbed it "Watergate Salad"—and the name stuck!

INGREDIENTS

1 (20-ounce) can crushed pineapple with juice, undrained

1 (3.4-ounce) package pistachio instant pudding mix

1 cup miniature marshmallows

½ cup chopped pecans

1 (8-ounce) container whipped topping, thawed, plus more for garnish, if desired

Chopped nuts, for garnish (optional)

DIRECTIONS

1. In a large bowl, combine the crushed pineapple, pudding mix, marshmallows, and pecans.

2. Fold in the whipped topping. Pour into an 8 × 8-inch baking dish.

3. Cover and chill for 4 hours or longer.

4. Top with additional whipped topping and chopped nuts, if desired. Slice or scoop portions onto plates. Serve.

Waldorf Salad

Yield: Serves 4 | Prep Time: 10 minutes | Chill Time: 1 hour

A popular entertaining dish, the Waldorf Salad was first created in the late nineteenth century by the maître d' of New York's famed Waldorf Hotel. I always make sure to grab a helping when I see it on the buffet line at a luncheon.

INGREDIENTS

2 tablespoons unsalted butter

2 tablespoons light brown sugar

½ cup pecans

2 red apples, cored and cut into chunks

2 celery stalks, thinly sliced

1 cup red seedless grapes, cut in half

2 tablespoons mayonnaise

2 tablespoons sour cream

Large lettuce leaves, for serving

DIRECTIONS

1. To make the candied pecans, melt the butter and brown sugar over medium heat. Once melted, add the pecans. Stir for 1 to 2 minutes, until coated. Transfer the pecans to a parchment paper–lined baking sheet to cool. Use a fork to separate the pecans.

2. In a medium bowl, combine the apples, celery, grapes, and candied pecans.

3. Fold in the mayonnaise and sour cream. Chill for 1 hour.

4. Line a platter or bowl with the lettuce leaves and top with the salad mixture.

Caesar Salad

Yield: Serves 6 | Prep Time: 15 minutes | Cook Time: N/A

While there are a few competing stories regarding the origins of the Caesar salad, rumor has it that it was popularized in the 1920s after it was allegedly created in a restaurant run by Caesar Cardini in Tijuana.

INGREDIENTS

Croutons

1 loaf crusty bread, cut into cubes

2 tablespoons olive oil

Kosher salt and freshly ground black pepper

Dressing

1 large egg

2–3 garlic cloves

1 teaspoon Dijon mustard

1–2 tablespoons Worcestershire sauce

4 anchovy fillets

Juice of 1–2 lemons

⅔ cup olive oil

¼ teaspoon freshly ground black pepper

¼ teaspoon red pepper flakes

Salad

2 heads romaine lettuce, rinsed, dried, and torn into pieces

½ cup grated Parmesan cheese

Freshly ground black pepper (optional)

DIRECTIONS

1. *For the croutons:* Preheat the oven to 400°F.

2. Place the bread cubes on a baking sheet. Drizzle with the olive oil and season with salt and pepper. Toss to coat.

3. Bake for 10 minutes, until the cubes are golden.

4. *For the dressing:* Fill a small saucepan with enough water to cover the egg and bring the water to a boil. Add the egg. Turn off the heat and let the egg sit for 1 to 2 minutes. Remove the egg.

5. In a blender, combine the garlic, mustard, Worcestershire sauce, anchovy fillets, and lemon juice. Process until smooth.

6. While the blender is running, add the olive oil a bit at a time until emulsified.

7. Add the coddled egg, black pepper, and red pepper flakes and process until thick.

8. *For the salad:* Place the lettuce in a large bowl. Add the dressing, using only enough to lightly coat the lettuce, and toss to coat.

9. Sprinkle with the Parmesan and top with the croutons.

10. Add a few grinds of black pepper and serve.

Sea Breeze Salad

Yield: Serves 10 to 12 | Prep Time: 10 minutes | Chill Time: 6-7 hours

Jell-O might be the ultimate vintage ingredient, and the Sea Breeze Salad is a throwback recipe that celebrates that. Refrigerators were still quite expensive up until World War II, so refrigeration-based recipes, like Jell-O salads, were still the ultimate status symbol. I especially love the bright yellow coloring with this recipe because it looks so pretty and cheery when I put it on the table.

INGREDIENTS

3 (3-ounce) packages lemon or lime Jell-O, or a combination of both

2 cups boiling water

2 cups cold water

1 (15-ounce) can lemon pie filling, or 1 (6-ounce) package Jell-O instant lemon pudding/pie filling mix, prepared according to package directions

1 cup drained crushed pineapple

2 cups whipped cream

DIRECTIONS

1. In a large bowl, dissolve the Jell-O mixes in the boiling water. Add the cold water and mix well. Chill according to the package instructions until thickened.

2. Stir the lemon pie filling or prepared lemon pudding into the thickened Jell-O and whip using a whisk or hand mixer until blended. Reserve 1 cup of the mixture.

3. Stir the pineapple into the remaining Jell-O mixture.

4. Pour into a 9 × 13-inch glass dish or decorative bowl. Refrigerate for 1 to 2 hours, until set.

5. Fold the reserved 1 cup Jell-O mixture into the whipped cream. Spread the mixture evenly over the Jell-O.

6. Chill for 1 hour or until set. Serve.

Ambrosia Salad

Yield: Serves 6 | Prep Time: 20 minutes | Chill Time: 2 hours

Ambrosia salad was a popular potluck dish in the '50s and '60s, serving double duty as both a side dish and a dessert. While this dish is more commonplace in the South, it's sure to earn raves all across the country.

INGREDIENTS

½ cup heavy cream

1 tablespoon confectioners' sugar

¼ cup sour cream

1 (20-ounce) can pineapple chunks, drained

1 (11-ounce) can mandarin oranges, drained and separated

½ cup maraschino cherries, drained and rinsed

1 cup green grapes, cut in half

1 small red apple, cored and cut into 1-inch chunks

1 cup mini marshmallows

1 cup sweetened flaked coconut

DIRECTIONS

1. In the bowl of a stand mixer fitted with the whisk attachment, beat the cream and confectioners' sugar on medium speed until it holds stiff peaks. Whisk in the sour cream. Set aside.

2. In a large bowl, combine the pineapple chunks, oranges, cherries, grapes, apple chunks, marshmallows, and coconut.

3. Fold in the sour cream mixture and toss to combine.

4. Chill for 2 hours. Serve.

Strawberry Pretzel Salad

Yield: Serves 10 to 12 | Prep Time: 50 minutes plus 2-4 hours chilling time | Cook Time: 10 minutes

Once the sugar shortages of World War II were over and refrigerators became less expensive, Jell-O once again entered the public eye with creative new recipes. TV ads in the '60s helped Jell-O reach its peak popularity, selling an average of four boxes per person per year. Snacks that party-goers could "nibble" on, such as pretzels, also reached the peak of their popularity during this time, so it was only natural that the two would be combined in this inventive recipe.

INGREDIENTS

1 (6-ounce) package strawberry Jell-O

2 cups boiling water

2½ cups salted pretzels

½ cup (1 stick) unsalted butter

¾ cup sugar

1 (8-ounce) package cream cheese, at room temperature

1 (8-ounce) tub whipped topping, thawed

1½ pounds fresh strawberries, hulled and sliced

DIRECTIONS

1. Preheat the oven to 350°F.

2. In a medium bowl, combine the Jell-O mix with the boiling water and stir for 2 minutes to completely dissolve. Set aside to cool.

3. Put the pretzels in a plastic zip-top bag and crush them using a rolling pin.

4. In a small saucepan, melt the butter, then add ¼ cup of the sugar and mix. Add the crushed pretzels and stir to combine.

5. Press the pretzel mixture evenly into a 9 × 13-inch glass baking dish.

6. Bake for 10 minutes, then set aside to cool.

7. In a medium bowl using a hand mixer, beat the cream cheese and the remaining ½ cup sugar until fluffy.

8. Fold in the whipped topping. Spread the mixture over the pretzel layer, making sure to cover the entire surface edge to edge. Cover and chill for 30 minutes.

9. Stir the strawberries into the cooled Jell-O. Carefully pour the mixture over the cream cheese layer.

10. Cover and refrigerate for 2 to 4 hours, until set. Cut into squares and serve.

Old-Fashioned Potato Salad

Yield: Serves 8 | Prep Time: 10 minutes | Cook Time: 15-20 minutes | Chill Time: 4 hours

While potato salads had been around for centuries, after Kraft introduced Miracle Whip in 1933 at the Century of Progress World's Fair in Chicago, they took on a whole new spin that perpetuated for decades. After the initial introductory period, Miracle Whip outsold all other brands of mayonnaise and was commonly used in different recipes. Feel free to use whatever brand of mayonnaise you'd like for this recipe, but if you want to go authentically retro with a sweeter and spicier taste, Miracle Whip is the way to go.

INGREDIENTS

2 pounds potatoes, cut into 1-inch chunks

1 cup Miracle Whip or mayonnaise

½ cup sour cream

1 tablespoon apple cider vinegar

1 tablespoon yellow mustard

1 teaspoon kosher salt

¼ teaspoon freshly ground black pepper

1 cup chopped celery

¼ cup chopped yellow onion

¼ cup chopped green onions

4 large hard-boiled eggs, chopped

DIRECTIONS

1. Bring a large stockpot of water to a boil. Add the potato chunks and cook for 15 to 20 minutes, until tender. Drain and reserve.

2. In a large bowl, whisk together the mayonnaise, sour cream, vinegar, mustard, salt, and pepper.

3. Add the potatoes, celery, yellow onion, and green onions and toss. Add the eggs and toss again.

4. Cover and chill for 4 hours or longer. Serve.

Monte Cristo

Yield: 1 sandwich | Prep Time: 10 minutes | Cook Time: 10 minutes

This classic sandwich was first served in Southern California in the 1950s and is still a staple on the lunch menu at Disneyland's Blue Bayou restaurant. Since it combines both breakfast and lunch ingredients, it's a great dish to serve for a weekend brunch.

INGREDIENTS

1 teaspoon mayonnaise

2 thick slices brioche bread

1 teaspoon grainy mustard

2 slices Jarlsberg cheese

2–3 ounces sliced smoked ham

1 large egg

1 tablespoon half-and-half

2 teaspoons unsalted butter

Confectioners' sugar, for sprinkling

Strawberry or raspberry preserves

DIRECTIONS

1. Spread the mayonnaise on one slice of bread. Spread the mustard on the other slice of bread.

2. Top each slice of bread with a slice of cheese. Add the ham on top of one of the slices and place the other piece of bread on top, cheese-side down.

3. In a small bowl, whisk the egg and half-and-half together.

4. In a small skillet, melt the butter over medium heat. Once the butter starts to sizzle, dip the sandwich into the egg and coat evenly on both sides.

5. Add the sandwich to the skillet and cook until brown, then flip and brown the other side, 2 to 3 minutes per side.

6. Serve warm, with a sprinkle of confectioners' sugar and a side of preserves.

Tuna Melt

Yield: 4 sandwiches | Prep Time: 15 minutes | Cook Time: 4-6 minutes per sandwich

There's a vintage diner in my town that my husband and I frequent on the weekends, and I swear they serve the most amazing tuna melt I've ever eaten. This recipe re-creates that magic with the perfect mix of veggies, seasonings, and plenty of tuna and melty cheese!

INGREDIENTS

2 (5-ounce) cans tuna, drained

½ small red onion, finely diced

½ celery stalk, finely diced

1 tablespoon minced fresh parsley

3 tablespoons mayonnaise

1 tablespoon horseradish mustard

1 tablespoon olive oil

½ teaspoon kosher salt

½ teaspoon freshly ground black pepper

8 slices sourdough bread

4 slices cheddar cheese

4 tablespoons (½ stick) unsalted butter, softened

DIRECTIONS

1. Place the tuna in a medium bowl and mash with a fork. Add the onion, celery, and parsley.

2. Add the mayonnaise, mustard, olive oil, salt, and pepper. Mix to combine.

3. Place two slices of bread on a clean work surface. Scoop 4 to 5 tablespoons of the tuna onto one slice of bread and top with 1 slice of cheese. Butter the second slice of bread and place on top.

4. In a medium skillet, melt ½ tablespoon of the butter over medium heat. Once the butter is sizzling, add the sandwich, butter-side up.

5. Cook for 2 to 3 minutes, until browned, then flip and cook on the second side for 2 to 3 minutes more, until browned.

6. Set the sandwich on a plate to cool slightly.

7. Repeat to make 3 more sandwiches. (You can also use a larger skillet and cook two sandwiches at a time.) Cut in half and serve.

Elvis's Favorite Sandwich

Yield: 4 sandwiches | Prep Time: 30 minutes | Cook Time: 2-3 minutes per sandwich

Elvis Presley was a cultural icon in the 1950s and '60s, and his legacy even spilled over into the culinary world. His love of peanut butter, bananas, and bacon is the stuff of legend, and once you try this sandwich, you'll see why!

INGREDIENTS

8 thick-cut bacon slices, chopped

1½ cups creamy peanut butter

½ cup (1 stick) unsalted butter, softened

2 tablespoons granulated sugar

8 thick slices brioche bread

4 bananas, sliced into ¼-inch-thick rounds

¼ cup packed dark brown sugar

DIRECTIONS

1. Cook the bacon in a large skillet over medium heat until crisp. Transfer to a paper towel–lined plate to cool. Pour the rendered bacon fat into a small bowl.

2. In another small bowl, stir together the bacon and the peanut butter.

3. In another small bowl, combine 6 tablespoons of the butter and the granulated sugar. Stir in 2 tablespoons of the reserved bacon fat. Spread the mixture on one side of each slice of bread.

4. Heat 2 tablespoons of the reserved bacon fat in the skillet used to fry the bacon. Add the bananas and brown sugar and cook until caramelized, 2 to 3 minutes.

5. Spread all 8 slices of bread with about 3 tablespoons of the peanut butter mixture.

6. Divide the bananas evenly on 4 of the peanut butter bread slices.

7. Press the remaining 4 bread slices on top.

8. Place ½ tablespoon butter in the skillet and let melt. Add the sandwich to the skillet and cook for 2 to 3 minutes until brown, then flip and brown the other side for 2 to 3 minutes more.

9. Set the sandwich on a wire rack to cool slightly.

10. Repeat with the remaining sandwiches. Cut in half and serve.

Patty Melt Sandwich

Yield: 4 sandwiches | Prep Time: 5 minutes | Cook Time: 35 minutes

The patty melt originated in Los Angeles at a restaurant chain owned by Biff and William "Tiny" Naylor in the 1940s and 1950s. The salty, cheesy sandwich was an instant hit and copycat recipes made their way onto diner menus throughout the country.

INGREDIENTS

2 tablespoons olive oil

Butter, for the pan (optional)

1 red onion, sliced

1 pound ground beef

1½ teaspoons kosher salt

½ teaspoon freshly ground black pepper

½ teaspoon garlic powder

½ teaspoon onion powder

½ teaspoon smoked paprika

2 teaspoons Worcestershire sauce

8 slices marbled rye bread

4 tablespoons (½ stick) unsalted butter, softened

8 slices Swiss cheese

8 slices American cheese

DIRECTIONS

1. Coat the bottom of a skillet with 1 tablespoon of the olive oil, or a mixture of olive oil and butter. Heat over medium-high heat until the oil is visibly hot; it will shimmer. Add the onion and stir to coat with the oil. Cook, stirring occasionally, until the onion begins to caramelize, about 20 minutes. Remove from the skillet and set aside.

2. In a large bowl, mix the ground beef, salt, pepper, garlic powder, onion powder, paprika, and Worcestershire sauce.

3. Divide the beef mixture into 4 balls. Flatten the balls into 4 patties about ¼ inch thick.

4. In a large skillet or on a griddle, heat the remaining 1 tablespoon olive oil over high heat. Cook the patties for 2 to 3 minutes on each side. Transfer the patties to a plate.

5. Wipe out the skillet.

6. Spread 3 tablespoons of the butter on one side of 4 slices of bread. Set aside.

7. On each of the remaining 4 slices of bread, place 2 slices of the Swiss cheese and 2 slices of the American cheese. Top each with a beef patty, then some caramelized onions. Top with a second slice of bread, butter-side up.

8. Melt the remaining 1 tablespoon butter in the skillet. Add two sandwiches to the skillet and cook until golden, then flip and brown the other side for 2 to 3 minutes more. Serve.

4

Sides

Side dishes could really make or break a meal back in the baby boomer era. While a meat dish usually took center stage, it was the sides that would bring the entire meal together and take dinnertime from average to memorable. I like making one or two of these on a Sunday (especially if it's a casserole) and then pairing them up with different dinners throughout the week. That way I can serve multiple dishes per meal without cooking several different dishes every night.

Red Hot Applesauce

Yield: 5 cups | Prep Time: 15 minutes | Cook Time: 60-80 minutes

When I was growing up, our next-door neighbors gave out jars of their homemade, retro-inspired red hot applesauce every year around Christmastime. It always looked so festive with its bright red coloring complementing the green ribbon around the jar. Those cinnamon red hots were first introduced in the 1930s, and once people realized they could be incorporated into gelatins and applesauce, they were an even bigger hit.

INGREDIENTS

5 pounds cooking apples (see Notes), peeled, cored, and cut into eighths

1½ cups apple cider

½–¾ cup sugar (see Notes)

1½ teaspoons vanilla extract

3 tablespoons candy red hots

¼ teaspoon kosher salt

DIRECTIONS

1. In a 6-quart stockpot, combine the apples, cider, sugar, vanilla, candy red hots, and salt. Stir. Cook over medium heat, stirring occasionally, until the mixture comes to a boil, about 18 minutes. Reduce the heat to the lowest simmer and cook, uncovered, for 45 to 60 minutes, until the apples are soft.

2. Use a wire potato masher to mash the apples to the consistency you like: less for slightly chunky applesauce and more for smooth. Or use an immersion blender to make a smooth sauce. Pour into bowls and serve.

NOTES

Cooking apples, like McIntosh or Empire, will make a sweeter sauce; add a tart apple, like Granny Smith, to make the flavor more complex. Depending on the type of apples used, the cook time will vary, so check after 40 minutes to determine how much longer to cook. The apples should be quite soft and easy to mash.

Different apples will also have different degrees of sweetness—remember that the red hots will add a bit of sugar as well. You may wish to use slightly less than ¾ cup sugar in the cooking process and taste after the sauce is mashed, adding a tablespoon or more as desired to the final product.

Easy Spanish Rice

Yield: Serves 4 to 6 | Prep Time: 5 minutes | Cook Time: 25-30 minutes

A favorite in Mexican restaurants, this recipe for Spanish rice serves as a side dish that can work with chicken, pork, and beef. Spanish rice gained mainstream popularity in the 1950s and '60s when magazine advertisements printed versions using quick-cook rice and canned tomatoes.

INGREDIENTS

1 tablespoon olive oil

½ cup chopped onion

1 tablespoon chopped jalapeño (optional)

1 teaspoon minced garlic

1 cup long-grain white rice (see Notes)

1 teaspoon chili powder

½ teaspoon ground cumin

½ teaspoon dried oregano

1 cup chicken broth

1 cup tomato sauce

1 cup frozen peas, thawed

1 tomato, diced

¼ cup salsa

Hot sauce, as desired

DIRECTIONS

1. In a medium pot, heat the olive oil over medium heat. Add the onion, jalapeño, and garlic and cook, stirring, for 1 minute, until aromatic. Add the rice and cook, stirring, for about 3 minutes, until the rice turns translucent. Add the chili powder, cumin, and oregano and stir for 1 minute more. Add the broth and tomato sauce and bring the mixture to a boil. Reduce the heat to maintain a simmer and cover. Cook for 20 to 25 minutes, until the rice is tender. Stir in the peas, remove from heat, and allow to sit for 5 minutes to heat the peas through.

2. Stir in the fresh tomato, salsa, and hot sauce to taste just before serving.

NOTES

If you choose to use a different variety of rice, adjust the cook time, and possibly the amount of liquid, according to the package directions.

Customize the heat level of this dish by using or omitting the jalapeño and by adding more or less hot sauce and mild or hot salsa in the end. Or allow the diners to add their own to suit their taste.

Broccoli Casserole

Yield: Serves 9 to 12 | Prep Time: 10 minutes | Cook Time: 50 minutes

Did you know that broccoli is an invented vegetable? It was actually bred by Italian farmers in the 1700s from several different kinds of cabbage! A member of the cruciferous veggie group along with cauliflower and turnips, this veggie made its way over to America in colonial times. It wasn't until the 1920s that it really gained in popularity, leading us to discover dishes like Broccoli Casserole that have become staples in the American diet to this day.

INGREDIENTS

1½ pounds fresh broccoli (about 8 cups)

½ cup (1 stick) unsalted butter

½ cup all-purpose flour

1 (12-ounce) can evaporated milk

½ teaspoon kosher salt

¼ teaspoon freshly ground black pepper

1½ cups grated Swiss cheese

1 cup sour cream

½ cup grated cheddar cheese

½ teaspoon paprika

1 (4-ounce) sleeve butter crackers, crushed

DIRECTIONS

1. Preheat the oven to 350°F. Coat a 9 × 13-inch baking dish with cooking spray.

2. Cut the broccoli florets into bite-size pieces and the tender stems into small dice. Place in a large microwaveable bowl, add ½ cup water, cover with plastic wrap, and microwave for about 5 minutes, until the broccoli is tender. Drain well and place in the prepared baking dish.

3. In a small saucepan, melt the butter over medium heat. Add the flour and whisk until the flour has been absorbed and the mixture turns light yellow with large dry bubbles. Add the evaporated milk, salt, and pepper and cook, whisking, until the sauce is thick and coats the back of a spoon, about 3 minutes. Add the Swiss cheese and sour cream and stir until the cheese has melted.

4. Pour the sauce over the broccoli in the baking dish and stir gently. Mix the cheddar cheese, paprika, and crackers and top the casserole in an even layer. Bake for about 40 minutes, until bubbling and the top is golden brown. Slice and serve.

Old-Fashioned Baked Mac 'n' Cheese

Yield: Serves 12 | Prep Time: 15 minutes | Cook Time: 50 minutes

I swear by homemade mac and cheese. I know that many people love the easy boxed version, but I remember the joy of eating the baked version, topped with a sprinkling of bread crumbs, when I was growing up. This particular recipe embodies 1950s home cooking because of the Velveeta cheese, a versatile, mild cheese popularized during the '30s, '40s, and '50s that produces a kid-friendly dish.

INGREDIENTS

1 pound elbow macaroni

2 teaspoons kosher salt, plus more for the pasta water

½ cup (1 stick) plus 6 tablespoons unsalted butter

½ cup all-purpose flour

2 teaspoons Dijon mustard

2 cups whole milk

2 cups half-and-half

½ teaspoon freshly ground black pepper

8 ounces Velveeta cheese, cut into cubes

1½ cups grated cheddar cheese

2 cups fresh bread crumbs

1 teaspoon paprika

DIRECTIONS

1. Preheat the oven to 350°F. Coat a 9 × 13-inch baking dish with cooking spray.

2. Bring a large pot of water to a boil. Add the macaroni and a dash of salt and cook according to the package directions until just al dente. Drain and place the pasta in a very large bowl.

3. While the pasta cooks, make the sauce. In a medium saucepan, melt ½ cup (1 stick) of the butter over medium heat. Add the flour and whisk until the flour has been absorbed and the mixture turns light yellow with large dry bubbles. Add the mustard, milk, half-and-half, salt, and pepper and cook, whisking, until the sauce is thick and coats the back of a spoon, about 3 minutes. Add the Velveeta and cheddar cheese and stir until the cheeses have melted and the sauce is smooth, about 5 minutes.

4. Pour the sauce over the cooked pasta and stir until completely coated. Place the pasta into the baking dish and smooth the top.

5. In a medium microwavable bowl, melt the remaining 6 tablespoons butter in the microwave. Stir in the bread crumbs and paprika until the mixture resembles wet sand. Sprinkle over the pasta and bake for about 30 minutes, until the casserole is bubbling and the top is light golden brown—do not overbake. Allow the casserole to cool for 5 minutes and serve.

Slow Cooker Green Bean Casserole

Yield: Serves 6 | Prep Time: 10 minutes | Cook Time: 4 hours on Low

I haven't always been a big fan of green beans, but as long as I can dress them up with ingredients like mushrooms and crunchy French fried onions, I'm first in line. French fried onions became a pantry staple in the 1950s, and the green bean casserole was the ideal vehicle to let them shine.

INGREDIENTS

1 pound fresh green beans, cut into 2-inch pieces

5 tablespoons unsalted butter

3 tablespoons all-purpose flour

½ cup chicken broth

½ cup whole milk

¼ cup half-and-half (or an additional ¼ cup whole milk)

6 ounces cremini mushrooms, stemmed and sliced

½ teaspoon kosher salt

¼ teaspoon freshly ground black pepper

½ cup finely grated Parmesan cheese

1 (2.8-ounce) container French fried onions

½ cup panko bread crumbs

DIRECTIONS

1. Coat the insert of a 6-quart slow cooker with cooking spray.

2. Put the green beans in the slow cooker.

3. In a small saucepan, melt 3 tablespoons of the butter over medium heat. Add the flour and whisk until the flour has been absorbed and the mixture turns light yellow with large dry bubbles. Add the broth, milk, and half-and-half and cook, whisking, until the sauce is thick and coats the back of a spoon, about 3 minutes.

4. In a medium skillet, melt 1 tablespoon of the butter over medium-high heat. Add the mushrooms and the salt and pepper and cook, stirring frequently, until they have exuded their liquids and begin to brown, 3 to 5 minutes. Remove from the heat.

5. Stir the Parmesan into the broth mixture and then stir in the mushrooms. Add 1 cup of the fried onions. Pour into the slow cooker and stir until the beans are coated. Cover and cook for 4 hours on Low.

6. When ready to serve, melt the remaining 1 tablespoon butter in a microwavable bowl, stir in the panko until the mixture resembles wet sand, and add the remaining fried onions. Spoon the topping over the cooked beans just before serving.

Dude Ranch Beans

Yield: Serves 4 | Prep Time: 10 minutes | Cook Time: 30 minutes

Dude ranches were the epitome of cowboy culture in the early twentieth century, and no food embodies the Wild West more than classic pork and beans. Cowboy Westerns filled the airwaves in the '50s, and kids grew up dreaming about the freedoms of living out west. While more so-phisticated dishes might be reserved for the adults, the kids would live out their cowboy fantasies with "real Western food" like beans and hot dogs.

INGREDIENTS

2 (15-ounce) cans pork and beans in tomato sauce

1 pound hot dogs

1 onion, cut into eighths

1 cup cherry or grape tomatoes

8 thick slices dill pickle

DIRECTIONS

1. Preheat the oven to 400°F. Coat an 8-inch round baking dish with cooking spray.

2. Pour the pork and beans into the baking dish.

3. Cut each hot dog into 1-inch pieces slightly on the diagonal. Thread eight 6-inch wooden skewers with alternating items: hot dog, onion, tomato, and pickle.

4. Lay the skewers over the beans in the baking dish and bake for 30 minutes. Serve.

Classic Corn Pudding

Yield: Serves 8 to 10 | Prep Time: 5 minutes | Cook Time: 40–50 minutes

In my family, somebody always makes sure to bring the corn pudding to Thanksgiving dinner. It's super easy to make, plus it's simple to transport. Corn pudding grew in popularity in the '50s and '60s thanks to magazine advertisements that encouraged home cooks to rework their pantry staples.

INGREDIENTS

1 (8.5-ounce) package corn muffin mix

½ cup (1 stick) unsalted butter, softened

2 large eggs

1 cup sour cream

½ cup whole milk

1 (15-ounce) can whole kernel corn, drained

1 (14-ounce) can creamed corn

DIRECTIONS

1. Preheat the oven to 325°F. Lightly coat a 9 × 13-inch baking dish with cooking spray.

2. In a large bowl, combine the corn muffin mix, butter, eggs, sour cream, and milk. Mix with a wooden spoon until just combined. Gently fold in the whole kernel corn and the creamed corn.

3. Pour into the baking dish and bake for 40 to 50 minutes, until the top is golden brown and the center is set.

VARIATIONS

If you prefer a sweeter corn pudding, consider adding up to ½ cup granulated sugar. I think the pudding is plenty sweet with the addition of the creamed corn, but it's just a bit more decadent with additional sugar.

Herb Garlic Popovers

Yield: 6 jumbo popovers or 12 regular popovers | Prep Time: 30 minutes, plus 1 hour resting time |
Cook Time: 50-55 minutes

Popovers were a big hit among home cooks in the 1950s. They were the quintessential from-scratch recipe that you'd see in advertisements for pantry staples like flour. It wasn't uncommon to give popover pans as an engagement or wedding present.

INGREDIENTS

3½ cups whole milk, at room temperature

4 cups all-purpose flour

1½ teaspoons kosher salt

1 teaspoon baking powder

6 large eggs, at room temperature

1 tablespoon fresh chives, minced

1 tablespoon fresh thyme, minced

1 teaspoon dried herbes de Provence

¼ teaspoon minced fresh garlic

1 cup grated Parmesan cheese

½ cup grated Asiago cheese

4 tablespoons (½ stick) unsalted butter, cut into 6 or 12 equal chunks, depending on how many popover cups you have in your tray, plus melted butter to grease the pan

DIRECTIONS

1. In a large saucepan, heat the milk over medium heat to 110°F.

2. In a large bowl, whisk together the flour, salt, and baking powder.

3. In the bowl of a stand mixer fitted with the whisk attachment, beat the eggs on low speed for 3 minutes. Add the warm milk and mix.

4. With the mixer running on low speed, slowly add the flour mixture. Once everything is combined, increase the speed to medium and beat for 2 minutes. Let the batter rest at room temperature for 1 hour.

5. While the batter is resting, in a separate medium bowl, mix the chives, thyme, herbes de Provence, and garlic. Add the Parmesan and Asiago cheeses. Set aside.

6. Preheat the oven to 450°F. Grease the popover pan with melted butter or coat with cooking spray. Place the popover pan on a baking sheet.

7. Pour the batter into the popover pan, filling the cups about three-quarters full. Sprinkle each popover with 1 tablespoon of the cheese-herb mixture. Top with a chunk of butter.

8. Bake for 15 minutes. Reduce the oven temperature to 375°F and bake for 30 to 35 minutes more, until the popovers are crispy and a dark golden brown. Do not open the oven until the popovers are done.

9. Remove the popovers and pierce with a sharp knife to let the steam escape. Let cool for 5 minutes and serve.

Classic Scalloped Potatoes

Yield: Serves 8 to 10 | Prep Time: 15 minutes | Cook Time: 1 hour 20 minutes

Julia Child had a popular version of this recipe during the first season of *The French Chef* in 1963, featured in the same infamous episode where Julia flipped part of a potato pancake onto the stovetop and scooped it right back into the pan. This version doesn't have as many seasonings as Julia's, but feel free to add thyme and other spices if you'd like to vary the dish.

INGREDIENTS

2 pounds Yukon Gold potatoes, cut into ¼-inch-thick slices

4 tablespoons (½ stick) unsalted butter

2 garlic cloves, finely grated

¼ cup all-purpose flour

1 teaspoon kosher salt

½ teaspoon freshly ground black pepper

3 cups whole milk

3 cups grated sharp cheddar cheese

DIRECTIONS

1. Preheat the oven to 425°F. Coat a 9 × 13-inch baking dish with cooking spray.

2. Fill a large bowl with cold water and place the potato slices in the water to prevent browning.

3. In a medium saucepan, melt the butter over medium-high heat. Add the garlic and cook for about 1 minute, until garlic is fragrant but not browning.

4. Add the flour, salt, and pepper and combine with the butter mixture using a whisk. Cook, stirring, for 5 minutes. The mixture will be thick.

5. Add the milk to the pot and cook, stirring with the whisk to ensure that there are no lumps. Increase the heat to high and bring to a boil. Cook, stirring with the whisk, for about 5 minutes, until the mixture thickens.

6. Remove the pot from the heat and add 2½ cups of the cheddar cheese. Stir, allowing the cheese to melt.

7. Layer half the potato slices evenly over the bottom of the prepared baking dish.

8. Pour half the cheese sauce mixture over the potato slices. Carefully spread the sauce evenly with a spatula.

9. Layer the remaining potato slices on top, followed by the remaining cheese sauce. Spread the sauce evenly as before. Sprinkle the top with the remaining ½ cup shredded cheese.

10. Bake for 1 hour, until the top is golden and the potatoes are tender.

11. Allow to cool for about 10 minutes before serving.

Peas Juliette

Yield: Serves 4 to 6 | Prep Time: 15 minutes | Cook Time: 25 minutes

Despite the familiar clichés about kids hiding their peas under mashed potato mounds to avoid the last dreaded bites, that notoriety may have been a function of their ubiquity: peas had been popular throughout the late nineteenth and early twentieth century and were among the first vegetables to ever be canned. They really saw a spike in interest, however, after the debut of the Jolly Green Giant in 1925. Modeled after a Brothers Grimm fairy tale, the Green Giant made his TV debut in 1959 and soon became the third most recognized ad icon of the twentieth century, according to *Advertising Age*.

INGREDIENTS

1 cup white rice

2 cups chicken broth or water

½ teaspoon kosher salt, plus more as needed

1 (15-ounce) can green peas

1 tablespoon cornstarch

3 tablespoons unsalted butter

¼ cup finely chopped onion

½ cup chopped canned pimento

Freshly ground black pepper

1 (5-ounce) can white chunk tuna in water, well drained

½ cup finely grated Parmesan cheese

½ cup finely chopped fresh parsley

DIRECTIONS

1. Coat a 4-cup Bundt pan or Jell-O mold with cooking spray.

2. In a medium saucepan, combine the rice, broth, and salt and cook according to the package directions for about 20 minutes.

3. Meanwhile, drain the peas and reserve the canning liquid in a small bowl. Add the cornstarch to the liquid and stir to dissolve.

4. In a small saucepan, melt the butter over medium heat. Add the onion and cook, stirring, until translucent, about 2 minutes. Add the broth mixture and the cornstarch mixture and stir continuously until the sauce thickens, about 2 minutes. Add the peas and pimento and cook until heated through. Taste and season with salt and pepper as desired.

5. When the rice is cooked, add the tuna, Parmesan, and parsley; stir well. Pack the hot mixture into the prepared Bundt pan or Jell-O mold, smoothing the top and pressing to firm up the rice. Immediately cover the mold with a serving plate and invert; carefully remove the pan. Spoon the peas over and around the rice and serve immediately.

NOTES

This is a recipe typical of those appearing on product labels in the '50s. If you wish to use frozen peas instead of the canned ones, replace the can juices with ¾ cup chicken broth and use 2 cups thawed frozen peas.

Easy Buttermilk Cornbread Muffins

Yield: 12 muffins | Prep Time: 10 minutes | Cook Time: 18-20 minutes

Buttermilk was a commonly used ingredient in cooking in the early and mid-twentieth century. In 1909, Americans consumed, on average, seven times more buttermilk than they do today. Once refrigerators with freezers heightened the appeal of frozen vegetables, such as corn, buttermilk cornbread muffins could be made all year long, not just when corn was in season.

INGREDIENTS

½ cup (1 stick) unsalted butter, melted

⅔ cup sugar

½ teaspoon baking soda

2 large eggs

1 cup buttermilk

1 cup cornmeal

1 cup all-purpose flour

½ teaspoon kosher salt

½ cup frozen corn kernels, thawed

Butter, for serving

DIRECTIONS

1. Preheat the oven to 375°F. Generously spray a 12-cup muffin tin with cooking spray.

2. In a medium bowl, combine the melted butter, sugar, and baking soda. Stir in the eggs, one at a time, until well blended. While stirring, slowly pour in the buttermilk. Do not overmix, and stop once the buttermilk is no longer visible.

3. Add the cornmeal, flour, and salt and stir until well combined. Fold in the corn kernels.

4. Fill each muffin cup about three-quarters full with the batter.

5. Bake for about 20 minutes, until the tops are lightly golden brown. Remove from the oven and allow to cool in the pan for 5 minutes. Turn the muffins out onto the board and serve with butter while warm.

Bundt Cake Noodle Ring

Yield: Serves 8 to 10 | Prep Time: 10 minutes | Cook Time: 45-50 minutes

Noodle rings peaked in popularity in the 1950s when home cooks started to acquire more light-weight metal and glassware. They were the type of dish you'd make to show off to friends and family, the star centerpiece in a buffet spread.

INGREDIENTS

1 (12-ounce) package egg noodles, cooked according to the package directions

1 (10¾-ounce) can each of cream of mushroom and chicken soup

1 cup sour cream

2 tablespoons unsalted butter, melted

1 tablespoon Worcestershire sauce

2 large eggs, beaten

2 cups shredded cheddar cheese

1 (12-ounce) bag frozen broccoli, thawed

1 (1-ounce) package onion soup mix

Kosher salt

DIRECTIONS

1. Preheat the oven to 350°F. Lightly coat a 10-inch Bundt pan with cooking spray.

2. In a large bowl, combine the egg noodles, cream of mushroom and chicken soup, sour cream, butter, Worcestershire sauce, eggs, cheddar cheese, broccoli, and onion soup mix. Stir until well combined. Taste and season with salt as needed. Spoon the mixture into the prepared Bundt pan, pressing down lightly.

3. Bake for 45 to 50 minutes, or until set and golden brown on top.

4. Let cool for at least 10 minutes, then carefully invert onto a platter, slice, and serve.

5

Dinner

In the 1950s and '60s, dinner was an event, a chance for the whole
family to gather around and talk about their days while enjoying
a meal that had been in the works for hours beforehand. In the
modern, fast-paced world we live in, moments like that become
increasingly rare, but I do always cherish those moments when I can
slow things down and appreciate the time I get to spend with my
family. Modern conveniences like slow cookers, premade ingredients,
and more make it feasible to enjoy these retro dishes any day.

No-Peek Chicken and Wild Rice Casserole

Yield: Serves 6 | Prep Time: 15 minutes | Cook Time: 1½ hours

Wild rice grew in popularity in the late 1960s, and soon, home cooks were finding great ways of working it into their recipes. For this particular casserole, make sure to keep the foil sealed nice and tight until after it's done baking to ensure it comes out perfectly cooked through.

INGREDIENTS

2 cups wild rice (about 14 ounces), uncooked

1 (10.5-ounce) can French onion soup

1 (10.5-ounce) can cream of chicken soup

1½ cups warm water

2 pounds boneless, skinless chicken breasts (see Notes)

⅓ container (6-ounce) French fried onions

¼ cup finely chopped fresh parsley

DIRECTIONS

1. Preheat the oven to 350°F. Coat a 9 × 13-inch baking dish with cooking spray.

2. In a large bowl, stir together the rice, French onion soup, cream of chicken soup, and warm water. Spread evenly into the prepared baking dish and lay the chicken breasts on top. Cover the dish with a double layer of aluminum foil and crimp the edges very tightly.

3. Bake for 90 minutes without peeking. Check to see that the rice is cooked (see Notes), and if not completely tender, return to the oven for a few minutes more.

4. Remove the foil and top the casserole with the French fried onions and parsley before serving.

NOTES

Use six 4-ounce chicken breasts; if only large breasts are available, use three and cut them crosswise to make six pieces before baking.

Rice mixes vary—those with more brown rice may require a longer cook time, so check after 90 minutes and re-cover and continue to bake if necessary. Buy a mix that is all rice without any seasoning packet or added ingredients.

Classic Meat Loaf

Yield: Serves 8 to 10 | Prep Time: 10 minutes | Cook Time: 1 hour 20 minutes

The '50s and '60s were a time to rediscover creativity in the kitchen, and meat loaf allowed home cooks to really stretch their wings. Have fun adapting this basic recipe to fit your every whim, from adding a mashed potato topping to switching out the meat used and much more!

INGREDIENTS

1½ pounds lean ground beef

¾ cup panko bread crumbs

½ cup whole milk

1 large egg, beaten

¼ cup finely diced onion

¼ cup finely diced carrot

¼ cup finely diced green bell pepper

Kosher salt and freshly ground black pepper

½ cup ketchup

¼ cup barbecue sauce

2 tablespoons light brown sugar

DIRECTIONS

1. Preheat the oven to 350°F. Lightly coat a loaf pan with cooking spray.

2. In a medium bowl, combine the ground beef, panko, milk, egg, onion, carrot, bell pepper, and salt and black pepper to taste. Gently mix all the ingredients together. Do not overmix or pack the meat too tightly.

3. Transfer the meat mixture to the prepared loaf pan and gently press evenly into the pan.

4. In a small bowl, mix together the ketchup, barbecue sauce, and brown sugar. Pour over the meat loaf.

5. Bake for 1 hour 20 minutes.

6. Remove from the oven and pour off any excess fat that has accumulated.

7. Allow to stand for 5 minutes before slicing and serving.

VARIATIONS

Add 1 cup grated cheese for a cheesy meat loaf.

NOTES

This can be made in the oven if desired. Use a 4- to 5-quart heavy casserole with lid. Cover the casserole and bake at 325°F for 3 to 4 hours until the beef is tender.

A good quality burgundy-style red wine is preferable here for the most authentic flavor.

Beef bourguignon is often served with steamed small red potatoes or can be served over wide egg noodles, if preferred.

Slow Cooker Beef Bourguignon

Yield: Serves 6 | Prep Time: 20 minutes | Cook Time: 6 hours on Low

Julia Child's *Mastering the Art of French Cooking* was a bestseller when it was released in the 1960s. One of her most famous recipes was the sophisticated French dish Beef Bourguignon. This savory dish is the essence of cozy comfort food, and this slow cooker version gets it just right.

INGREDIENTS

3 pounds beef stew meat, cut into 2-inch cubes

2 tablespoons all-purpose flour

1 teaspoon kosher salt

¼ teaspoon freshly ground black pepper

4 bacon slices, cut into 1-inch pieces

1 tablespoon olive oil

1 teaspoon finely minced garlic

1 pound cremini mushrooms, stemmed and quartered

3 cups red wine (see Notes)

2 cups beef broth

1 tablespoon tomato paste

3 carrots, sliced

1½ cups pearl onions (thawed if frozen; peeled and trimmed if fresh)

3 sprigs fresh thyme

1 small bay leaf

DIRECTIONS

1. Coat the insert of an 8-quart slow cooker with cooking spray.

2. Place the beef stew meat in a large zip-top bag and add the flour, salt, and pepper. Close the bag and shake vigorously to completely coat the meat.

3. In a large skillet or stockpot, brown the bacon over medium heat until cooked but not crisp. Remove the bacon, leaving the fat in the pan. Add half the olive oil and the beef in batches (do not crowd the pan) and cook over medium-high heat, turning to brown all sides. Transfer the meat to the slow cooker as it browns, add the remaining olive oil as necessary, and cook until all the beef has been browned and transferred to the slow cooker. Reserve the flour that remains in the bag.

4. Reduce the heat to medium and add the garlic. Cook for about 1 minute, until aromatic. Add the mushrooms and cook, stirring, until the mushrooms have released their moisture and begin to brown slightly, about 2 minutes. Raise the heat to medium-high, add the flour from the plastic bag, and stir for 1 minute, until the flour has been absorbed. Add ¼ cup of the wine to the pan and cook, stirring to scrape up any browned bits from the bottom of the pan. Add the remaining wine and the broth and bring to a simmer. Stir in the tomato paste and pour the mixture into the slow cooker over the beef. Add the carrot, pearl onions, bacon, thyme sprigs, and bay leaf; cover and cook for 6 hours on Low. Remove the bay leaf. Ladle into bowls and serve.

Turkey Tetrazzini

Yield: Serves 10 to 12 | Prep Time: 15 minutes | Cook Time: 30 minutes

Frozen foods were given a boost of popularity in the 1950s when refrigerators with freezers became affordable enough for many households to have in-house, especially when Swanson introduced the frozen TV dinner in 1954. Frozen peas and other frozen veggies became commonplace.

INGREDIENTS

1 pound fettuccine

2 tablespoons olive oil

4 cups shredded cooked turkey, light and dark meat

2 cups frozen peas

6 tablespoons (¾ stick) unsalted butter

1 cup finely chopped onion

½ cup finely chopped celery

8 ounces cremini mushrooms, stemmed and thinly sliced

1 teaspoon kosher salt

1 teaspoon dried sage or poultry seasoning

¼ cup sherry

⅓ cup all-purpose flour

3 cups chicken broth

2 cups whole milk or half-and-half

½ cup fine dried bread crumbs

½ cup finely grated Parmesan cheese

½ teaspoon paprika

2 tablespoons unsalted butter, melted

DIRECTIONS

1. Preheat the oven to 375°F. Coat a 9 × 13-inch baking dish with cooking spray.

2. Bring a large pot of water to a boil. Add the fettuccine and cook until just al dente. Drain and return to the pot. Toss with 1 tablespoon of the olive oil. Stir in the turkey and peas and set aside.

3. While the pasta cooks, in a large deep skillet, heat the remaining 1 tablespoon olive oil and half of the butter over medium heat. Add the onion and celery and cook, stirring, about 2 minutes. Add the mushrooms, salt, and sage and cook, stirring, until the mushrooms begin to brown slightly, about 2 minutes.

4. Pour in the sherry and stir. Cook for 1 minute, until the liquid has nearly evaporated. Remove the vegetables. Add the remaining 3 tablespoons butter and let it melt, then sprinkle the flour into the pan and cook, stirring, about 1 minute. Gradually add the broth, stirring continuously, and when the mixture begins to thicken, add the milk and cook, stirring, until the sauce is thickened, about 5 minutes total.

5. Remove the skillet from the heat and pour the sauce over the pasta. Stir in the mushroom mixture and pour into the baking dish.

6. In a small bowl, combine the bread crumbs, Parmesan, and paprika with the melted butter. Sprinkle evenly over the pasta mixture. Bake for 30 minutes, or until the casserole is heated through and bubbling, and the top is golden brown. Allow it to cool for 5 minutes and serve.

Very Best Salisbury Steak

Yield: Serves 4 | Prep Time: 15 minutes plus 30 minutes chilling time | Cook Time: 20 minutes

TV dinners first made their mark in the early 1950s, and as families began to pair dinner and their favorite TV shows, like *I Love Lucy* and *Dragnet*, meals like Salisbury steak rose into prominence. Don't worry, though—just because this version is homemade doesn't mean you can't still eat it in front of the TV.

INGREDIENTS

Beef Patties

1 pound lean ground beef

¼ cup fine dried bread crumbs

2 tablespoons tomato paste

1 tablespoon Worcestershire sauce

½ teaspoon kosher salt

¼ teaspoon freshly ground black pepper

1 tablespoon olive oil

Sauce

1 tablespoon olive oil

1 cup finely diced onion

4 ounces mushrooms, sliced

1 tablespoon fresh thyme, or 1 teaspoon dried

3 tablespoons all-purpose flour

2 cups beef broth

1 tablespoon Worcestershire sauce

1 teaspoon tomato paste

Kosher salt and freshly ground black pepper

DIRECTIONS

1. *For the beef patties:* In a large bowl, combine the ground beef, bread crumbs, tomato paste, Worcestershire sauce, salt, and pepper and mix well, using your hands, until the mixture is very well blended and almost smooth in texture. Form into 4 oval patties ½ inch thick and press a "dimple" into the top of each. Chill for 30 minutes.

2. In a large skillet, heat the olive oil over medium-high heat. Add the patties and cook until nearly cooked through and browned, about 4 minutes on each side. Set aside on a plate and keep warm.

3. *For the sauce:* In the same pan, heat the olive oil over medium-high heat. Add the onion and cook, stirring, until translucent, about 2 minutes. Add the mushrooms and thyme and cook, stirring, until the mushrooms release their moisture and begin to brown slightly. Sprinkle with the flour and cook, stirring, until the flour has been absorbed, about 1 minute. Gradually add the broth, Worcestershire, and tomato paste while stirring and loosening any browned bits from the bottom of the pan, and let the sauce come to a simmer until it is thickened slightly.

4. Return the beef to the pan with the sauce and cook at a simmer for 8 to 10 minutes more, flipping halfway through, until the beef is completely cooked. Taste and season with salt and pepper, if necessary.

5. Drizzle the meat with the sauce and serve.

Homemade Chicken Potpie

Yield: Serves 6 to 8 │ Prep Time: 15 minutes │ Cook Time: 40-45 minutes

Around the same time that prepackaged frozen meals started making their way into supermarkets, the Swanson brothers began manufacturing frozen chicken and turkey potpies, which were an instant hit. This version takes a little more work than popping a ready-made dish in the oven, but once you try the flaky crust and creamy chicken and broth, you won't have any regrets.

INGREDIENTS

2 tablespoons unsalted butter

3 tablespoons all-purpose flour

½ teaspoon poultry seasoning

½ teaspoon kosher salt

¼ teaspoon freshly ground black pepper

1½ cups chicken broth

2 cups cooked chicken, cut into ½-inch cubes (see Note)

1 (12-ounce) bag frozen peas and carrots, thawed

1 tablespoon finely chopped fresh parsley

1 large egg

1 teaspoon heavy cream or whole milk

1 prepared pie crust

DIRECTIONS

1. Preheat the oven to 375°F. Coat a 9-inch deep-dish pie plate with cooking spray.

2. In a large deep skillet, melt the butter over medium-high heat. Sprinkle with the flour, poultry seasoning, salt, and pepper and cook, stirring, for 1 to 2 minutes, until the flour has been absorbed. Gradually stir in the broth and cook, stirring, for 3 to 4 minutes, until the sauce is thick. Stir in the chicken, frozen peas and carrots, and parsley. Pour into the prepared pie plate.

3. In a small bowl, beat the egg. Pour about half the egg over the mixture in the pie plate and stir to mix. Stir the cream into the remaining egg in the bowl and set aside.

4. Place the pie crust on top of the pie plate and crimp the edges to seal. Use a pastry brush to brush the egg-milk mixture on top of the crust and cut several slits to allow steam to escape. Bake for 40 to 45 minutes, until the potpie is bubbling and the crust is golden brown. Slice and serve.

NOTE

To cook the chicken, place 2 medium boneless, skinless chicken breasts on a baking sheet and bake at 350°F for 30 minutes.

Simple Tuna Croquettes

Yield: Serves 4 | Prep Time: 5 minutes | Cook Time: 8-10 minutes

Tuna didn't find its footing in American cuisine until after it began being sold in cans in 1908. It was branded as Chicken of the Sea to add a sense of familiarity, and soon became America's most consumed fish and was commonly used in many family recipes like tuna noodle casserole and tuna croquettes. While tartar sauce has been around since the 1800s, it rose in the public eye in 1947 after the Mazola company began taking out four-page color advertising spreads in magazines, extolling the pairing of tartar sauce and fish.

INGREDIENTS

Tartar Sauce

½ cup mayonnaise

2 tablespoons sweet pickle relish

1 teaspoon lemon zest

2 teaspoons fresh lemon juice

½ teaspoon cayenne pepper or paprika

Salt and freshly ground black pepper

Croquettes

2 large eggs

1½ cups panko bread crumbs

½ cup whole milk

¼ cup all-purpose flour

2 tablespoons green onion, chopped finely, including some of the tender green tops

½ teaspoon kosher salt

1 (5-ounce) can solid tuna packed in water, very well drained

2 teaspoons paprika or cayenne pepper

Vegetable oil, for frying

DIRECTIONS

1. *For the tartar sauce:* In a small bowl, combine the mayonnaise, relish, lemon zest, lemon juice, cayenne, salt, and pepper. Stir well and set aside.

2. *For the croquettes:* In a large bowl, stir together the eggs, ½ cup of the bread crumbs, the milk, flour, green onion, and salt until well blended. Add the tuna and 1 teaspoon of the paprika and stir very well with a fork, breaking up the fish into very small pieces. Let stand for 5 to 10 minutes.

3. Meanwhile, in a deep skillet or wok, heat 2 inches of vegetable oil over medium-high heat to 350°F.

4. In a small bowl, combine the remaining 1 cup panko and 1 teaspoon paprika.

5. Use two spoons or an ice cream scoop to divide the tuna mixture into 8 portions and drop each into the bowl of crumbs, turning gently to coat all sides.

6. When the oil is hot, fry the croquettes in batches until golden brown, about 4 minutes. Scoop from the oil onto layers of paper towels to drain while you finish frying the rest. Serve hot, with the tartar sauce on the side.

Honey-Glazed Spiral Ham

Yield: Serves 6 | Prep Time: 10 minutes | Cook Time: 2½ hours

In the 1950s and '60s, large roasted meats were the most efficient way to feed the entire family. Plus, you'd wind up with plenty of leftovers that you could use in sandwiches or cook into other meals, so it was a win-win.

INGREDIENTS

1 (3-pound) spiral cut ham

1 cup fresh orange juice

¼ cup honey

¼ cup packed light brown sugar

1 tablespoon Worcestershire sauce

Zest of 1 orange

DIRECTIONS

1. Preheat oven to 325°F. Coat a lidded 6-quart Dutch oven with cooking spray.

2. Prepare and cook the ham according to the directions on the label.

3. While the ham bakes, prepare the glaze. In a medium saucepan, combine the orange juice, honey, brown sugar, and Worcestershire sauce and bring to a boil over medium heat. Boil for 2 minutes. Reduce the heat to maintain a simmer and cook the mixture until thick and bubbling, about 7 minutes. Remove from the heat and add the orange zest.

4. Remove the ham from the oven. Brush the glaze over the hot ham, allowing the juices to get between the slices. Return to the oven and bake for 10 to 15 minutes more. Serve with any remaining glaze.

Farmer's Pork Chops

Yield: Serves 4 | Prep Time: 20 minutes | Cook Time: 1 hour 15 minutes

"Meat and potatoes" are said to be the classic country-style dinner combination when you're just looking to kick back and enjoy some down-home cooking. Pork itself saw a spike in popularity in the 1960s when bacon was sold for 65 cents per pound, 20 cents cheaper than steak. This dinner recipe combines hearty potatoes with tender pork chops with a hint of onion and seasonings. Feel free to peel the potatoes or leave them unpeeled, whichever you prefer!

INGREDIENTS

1 cup all-purpose flour

1 teaspoon steak seasoning

4 (½-inch-thick) pork chops, trimmed of excess fat

2 pounds Yukon Gold potatoes

1 cup sliced onion

½ cup (1 stick) unsalted butter

½ teaspoon kosher salt

¼ teaspoon cayenne pepper

2 cups whole milk or rich chicken broth

2 tablespoons vegetable oil

DIRECTIONS

1. Preheat the oven to 350°F. Coat a 3-quart oval or rectangular microwaveable baking dish with cooking spray.

2. Place ½ cup of the flour and the steak seasoning in a large zip-top bag and shake well. Add the pork chops and shake to coat the chops evenly with the flour. Set aside.

3. Scrub and slice the potatoes, piercing them with a fork to vent, and arrange in the prepared baking dish in an even layer. Arrange the onion slices on top. Cover with plastic wrap and microwave for about 5 minutes, until the potatoes can be pierced with the tip of a knife but are not completely cooked.

4. While the potatoes cook, in a small saucepan, melt the butter over medium heat. Whisk in the remaining ½ cup flour, the salt, and the cayenne and cook, stirring, until bubbles form and the mixture turns light yellow, about 2 minutes. Slowly add the milk and cook, stirring, for 2 minutes more, until the sauce thickens and coats the back of a spoon. Pour the sauce over the potatoes and shake the baking dish to distribute it evenly.

5. In a skillet large enough to hold all the chops at once, heat the vegetable oil over medium-high heat. Shake the chops to remove any excess flour and cook for 4 minutes on each side, or until golden brown but not completely cooked. Arrange the chops on top of the potatoes and bake, uncovered, for 1 hour. Serve.

Easy Beef Stroganoff

Yield: Serves 4 | Prep Time: 10 minutes | Cook Time: 45 minutes

This dish was first introduced in the mid-nineteenth century and really picked up steam after the start of World War II. It's gotten fancied up over the years—originally, the dish didn't include mushrooms or onions—but the same basic principles are still there, as beloved as ever.

INGREDIENTS

½ teaspoon kosher salt, plus more for the water

3 tablespoons olive oil

1½ pounds sirloin steak, cut into thin ½ × 2-inch strips (see Note)

¼ teaspoon freshly ground black pepper

1 onion, sliced lengthwise into thin slices

1 teaspoon finely minced garlic

½ cup finely chopped fresh parsley

1 pound button mushrooms, stemmed and quartered

¼ cup all-purpose flour

¼ cup dry white wine

1 pound wide egg noodles

2 cups beef broth

2 tablespoons Worcestershire sauce

½ cup sour cream, plus extra for serving

DIRECTIONS

1. Bring a large pot of salted water to a boil.

2. In a large nonstick skillet, heat half the oil over medium-high heat. Season the strips of steak with the salt and pepper and place flat-side down on the skillet. Cook without moving until nicely browned, about 3 minutes. Turn and cook the second flat side for 2 to 3 minutes, until well browned. Transfer to a bowl and set aside. If all the meat does not fit into the pan at one time, work in two batches.

3. Add the remaining oil to the pan. Add the onion and cook, stirring frequently, for 2 minutes. Add the garlic and half the parsley, stir for 1 minute, then add the mushrooms and cook, stirring frequently, until the mushrooms have slightly browned and the liquids have evaporated.

4. Sprinkle the flour over the mushrooms and cook, stirring, for 1 minute, or until the flour has been absorbed. Add the wine and cook, stirring to scrape up any browned bits from the bottom of the pan, until the wine has reduced by half, 2 to 3 minutes.

5. Drop the egg noodles into the pot of boiling water and cook for 6 to 7 minutes or as the package directs, then drain.

6. Meanwhile, add the broth and Worcestershire sauce to the skillet, reduce the heat to medium, and stir frequently to form a slightly thickened sauce, about 5 minutes. Finally, stir in the sour cream until smooth, then return the meat to the pan just until reheated, 1 minute.

7. Serve the stroganoff over the noodles, top with sour cream, and sprinkle with the remaining chopped parsley.

NOTE

Put the steak in the freezer
for 20 minutes to make it
easier to slice.

Reliable Chicken and Dumplings

Yield: Serves 6 to 8 | Prep Time: 30 minutes | Cook Time: 20 minutes

One of the largest waves of immigration to the United States occurred between 1880 and 1920. By the 1950s and '60s, many of these immigrants had merged their culinary traditions into American cuisine. This eastern European recipe for chicken and dumplings soon became synonymous with American comfort food and remains so to this day.

INGREDIENTS

1 pound chicken breasts, boneless or bone-in

½ cup chopped onion

¼ cup chopped fresh parsley, plus more for garnish

1 bay leaf

1 teaspoon kosher salt, plus more as needed

2 cups plus 2 tablespoons all-purpose flour

½ teaspoon baking powder

2 tablespoons cold unsalted butter, cut into bits

About ¾ cup whole milk

Freshly ground black pepper

DIRECTIONS

1. Place the chicken in a Dutch oven and add 2½ quarts water, onion, parsley, bay leaf, and salt. Bring to a low boil, reduce the heat to maintain a simmer, and cook for 25 minutes. Remove the chicken and shred into bite-size pieces, discarding any bone and skin. Strain the broth and measure 2 quarts (add water if necessary to reach 2 quarts).

2. Return the broth to the same Dutch oven (no need to wash) and bring to a low simmer.

3. Meanwhile, in a food processor, pulse 2 cups of the flour, the baking powder, and the butter together until crumbly. With the motor running, slowly add the milk until the dough clumps together—you may not need the entire amount of milk.

4. On a work surface lightly dusted with the remaining 2 tablespoons of flour, scoop the dough from the processor into a rough disc and roll into a rectangle ¼ inch thick. Cut the dough into 2-inch squares.

5. Meanwhile, increase the heat under the pot of broth so the mixture boils, add the chicken, then drop in the squares of dough a few at a time, stirring so they do not stick together. Once all the dumplings are in the pot, cook, occasionally stirring gently, for 20 minutes, or until the dumplings no longer have a raw, floury look.

6. Taste the broth to see if it needs additional salt and pepper, then serve in soup bowls, garnished with more chopped parsley.

Homemade Sloppy Joes

Yield: 8 sandwiches | Prep Time: 10 minutes | Cook Time: 20-30 minutes

While sloppy joes have been around for many decades, they really started to surge in popularity after the Manwich brand released a sloppy joe sauce in 1969. This economic dish continued to make its way into the mainstream, eventually becoming the signature lunchroom dish we know and love.

INGREDIENTS

1 pound lean ground beef

½ cup finely chopped onion

½ cup finely chopped green bell pepper

1 teaspoon finely minced garlic (optional)

1 (14-ounce) can diced tomatoes, undrained

2 tablespoons bottled chili sauce

1 tablespoon light brown sugar

1 tablespoon yellow mustard

½ teaspoon kosher salt

8 hamburger buns

Sliced sweet pickles (optional)

Potato chips, for serving

DIRECTIONS

1. In a large skillet, crumble the beef and brown it over medium-high heat, breaking up any clumps, for about 3 minutes. Add the onion, bell pepper, and garlic (if using) and cook, stirring, for 2 minutes more.

2. In a medium bowl, combine the tomatoes and their juices, the chili sauce, brown sugar, mustard, and salt. Add the tomato mixture to the skillet and bring the mixture to a low boil. Reduce the heat to low and partially cover the pan. Simmer, stirring once or twice, until the mixture begins to thicken, about 20 minutes.

3. Meanwhile, preheat the broiler.

4. Toast the hamburger buns under the broiler until the cut sides are golden. Spoon the meat mixture onto the buns and garnish with pickle slices and potato chips to serve.

Creamed Chicken on Waffles

Yield: Serves 4 | Prep Time: 15 minutes | Cook Time: 20 minutes

Unlike today, where waffles are almost always served during breakfast, from the '30s through the '50s, it was common to see waffles served alongside different meats or vegetables for dinner. While waffles for dinner still appear in Southern cuisine, this dish has the throwback vintage charm of an oft-forgotten favorite.

INGREDIENTS

Waffles

1 (8.5-ounce) package corn bread mix

1 large egg

½ cup whole milk

2 tablespoons vegetable oil

Topping

4 tablespoons (½ stick) unsalted butter

¾ cup finely chopped onion

½ cup finely diced carrot

⅓ cup finely diced celery

¼ cup all-purpose flour

1½ cups whole milk or half-and-half

½ teaspoon kosher salt

⅛ teaspoon poultry seasoning or dried thyme

3 cups cubed cooked chicken breast (see Note)

½ cup frozen peas, thawed

DIRECTIONS

1. Preheat a Belgian electric waffle iron. Preheat the oven to 200°F.

2. *For the waffles:* In a small bowl, combine the corn bread mix, egg, milk, and vegetable oil and whisk until smooth. Set aside while the waffle iron heats.

3. *For the topping:* In a small saucepan, melt the butter over medium heat. Add the onion, carrot, and celery and cook, stirring, until the vegetables are softened, about 4 minutes. Sprinkle the flour over the vegetables and cook, stirring, until the flour has been completely absorbed, about 1 minute. Gradually stir in the milk, salt, and poultry seasoning and cook, stirring, until the mixture has thickened, about 3 minutes. Pour into an oven-safe dish.

4. Stir the cooked chicken and peas into the topping and keep warm in the heated oven.

5. Use half the waffle mixture to make the first waffle, following the manufacturer's instructions. Remove the waffle and transfer it to the oven to keep warm while you make the second waffle.

6. To serve, place two quarters of each waffle on each serving plate and top with a scoop of the chicken mixture. Serve immediately.

NOTE

To cook the chicken, place 3 medium boneless, skinless chicken breasts on a baking sheet and bake at 350°F for 30 minutes. Cut into cubes.

Slow Cooker Roast Beef

Yield: Serves 6 | Prep Time: 10 minutes | Cook Time: 5 hours

In 1947, Americans set a record for meat consumption with an average of 155 pounds eaten per person per year. In 1948, however, prices were so high that consumers boycotted butcher shops, causing prices to drop by as much as 20 percent to lure consumers back. Beef was the preferred meat after World War II, beating out pork and lamb by a long shot. Roasts, like this one, were fitting for special occasions or Sunday-night dinners, especially with the possibility of leftovers to enjoy.

INGREDIENTS

4 sprigs fresh rosemary, plus more for garnish

1 tablespoon chopped garlic

1 teaspoon coarse salt

1 tablespoon Worcestershire sauce

3 tablespoons olive oil

1 (2-pound) eye of round beef roast

DIRECTIONS

1. Coat the insert of an 8-quart slow cooker with cooking spray.

2. Pluck the leaves from the rosemary to measure 2 tablespoons. Lay the stems with any remaining leaves in the bottom of the slow cooker.

3. On a work surface, stack the rosemary leaves, garlic, and salt and mince together to form a smooth paste. In a small bowl, combine this paste with the Worcestershire sauce and 2 tablespoons of the olive oil. Rub and pat this mixture on all sides of the roast, including the ends.

4. In a large skillet, heat the remaining 1 tablespoon olive oil over high heat. Add the roast and cook, turning to brown all sides to a lightly browned crust, about 4 minutes total. Place the roast in the slow cooker over the rosemary sprigs, cover, and cook on Low for 5 hours or until cooked to your desired doneness. Use an internal thermometer to test—the center of the roast should register 150°F for medium.

5. Remove from the slow cooker and let stand for 10 minutes before slicing, garnishing with fresh rosemary sprigs, and serving.

Buttermilk Fried Chicken

Yield: Serves 4 | Prep Time: 20 minutes | Cook Time: 35 minutes

In the mid-1900s, methods of chicken farming were dramatically scaled up, which meant that the now ubiquitous poultry became a more frequent occurrence on dinner menus. Around this time, fast food joints started to really take off, and with the launch of Kentucky Fried Chicken, fried chicken found a national audience after years of being a Southern staple.

INGREDIENTS

1 pound chicken wings

3 cups buttermilk

1 tablespoon hot sauce

2 cups all-purpose flour

Kosher salt and freshly ground black pepper

1 teaspoon baking soda

2 teaspoons baking powder

2 large eggs

Vegetable oil, for frying

DIRECTIONS

1. Pat the chicken dry with paper towels.

2. In a large bowl, mix the buttermilk and hot sauce. Add the chicken to the buttermilk mixture and allow to sit while prepping the remaining ingredients, or up to 1 hour.

3. In a shallow dish, combine the flour, salt, pepper, baking soda, and baking powder.

4. In a separate shallow dish, mix the eggs and ¼ cup water.

5. To prepare the chicken, work as follows: First dredge the chicken in the flour mixture, then dip into the egg mixture. Dredge the chicken in the flour mixture once more. Place the chicken on a plate and repeat to coat all the chicken pieces.

6. In a large heavy-bottomed skillet, heat at least 1 inch of vegetable oil over medium-high heat. Add the chicken to the pan carefully, no more than 4 pieces at a time. Cook for about 7 minutes, then flip. Cook the second side for 3 to 5 minutes, until the chicken is cooked through. Remove the chicken from the oil and place it on paper towels to drain, and sprinkle with salt while hot. Repeat with the remaining chicken pieces.

7. Serve immediately.

Old-Fashioned Tuna Noodle Casserole

Yield: Serves 8 | Prep Time: 10 minutes | Cook Time: 35 minutes

When I think of versatile casseroles, my mind immediately jumps to tuna casseroles. Not only are they a welcome dinner option—even for picky eaters—but they're easy to make and store in the freezer. Ready-made ingredients like cream of mushroom soup added flavor and moisture while beloved crispy toppings of the era like French fried onions and potato chips added texture.

INGREDIENTS

2 tablespoons unsalted butter

½ cup diced onion

1 (10.5-ounce) can cream of mushroom soup

½ cup mayonnaise

½ cup sour cream

⅓ cup whole milk

½ teaspoon kosher salt

½ teaspoon freshly ground black pepper

12 ounces wide egg noodles, cooked

1 (12-ounce) can solid white albacore tuna in water, drained well

1 cup frozen peas

1½ cups shredded cheddar cheese

⅓ container (6-ounce) French fried onions

DIRECTIONS

1. Preheat the oven to 350°F. Coat a 9 × 13-inch baking dish with cooking spray.

2. In a skillet, melt the butter over medium heat. Add the onion and cook, stirring, until tender and translucent, about 5 minutes.

3. In a large bowl, combine the cream of mushroom soup, mayonnaise, sour cream, milk, salt, pepper, and the cooked onions and butter from the skillet. Mix well.

4. Add the noodles, tuna, peas, and cheddar cheese. Gently fold the mixture until well blended. Pour the mixture into the prepared baking dish. Top evenly with the fried onions.

5. Bake for about 30 minutes, until the casserole is bubbling and the topping is beginning to brown lightly. Serve.

Country Fried Steak

Yield: Serves 6 | Prep Time: 10 minutes | Cook Time: 20 minutes

Chicken fried steak and country fried steak have been staples of Texas cuisine since the early 1950s. This dish uses very few ingredients, making it both budget-friendly and super simple.

INGREDIENTS

3 cups whole milk

2 large eggs

2 cups all-purpose flour

½ teaspoon garlic powder

Kosher salt and freshly ground black pepper

2 pounds cube steak

Vegetable oil

Mashed potatoes, for serving (optional)

Peas, for serving (optional)

DIRECTIONS

1. In a shallow dish, whisk together 1 cup of the milk and the eggs. In another shallow dish, mix together 1¾ cups of the flour, the garlic powder, and salt and pepper. Set the dish with the milk and eggs and the dish with the flour mixture next to each other. Set a wire rack on a baking sheet to hold the coated meat and set it next to the flour mixture.

2. To coat the steak, dip it first in the egg mixture, then into the flour mixture. Next dip the steak back into the egg mixture, then finally the flour mixture. Place the coated meat on the rack. Repeat with the remaining pieces of steak.

3. While the meat rests, heat at least 1 inch of vegetable oil in a large skillet over medium-high heat. Cook the meat two pieces at a time, about 3 minutes per side. The edges of the meat will begin to turn a golden brown. Once the steak is cooked on both sides, transfer it to a rack set over a paper towel–lined baking sheet. Repeat with the remaining steaks.

4. While the meat is resting, carefully drain all but ¼ cup of the oil from the pan. Return the pan to the heat and allow to warm back up.

5. Whisk the remaining ¼ cup flour into the oil and continue stirring while cooking the flour mixture. Allow the mixture to become golden brown.

6. While continuing to whisk, pour in the remaining 2 cups milk. Keep stirring until the mixture thickens, adding more milk if it becomes too thick. Taste and season with salt and pepper. Cook for 5 minutes more, until the gravy is thick.

7. To serve, place the steak on a plate and top with gravy. Serve with mashed potatoes and peas, if desired.

Chicken à la King

Yield: Serves 4 | Prep Time: 10 minutes | Cook Time: 20 minutes

This dish was an elegant dinner recipe often found at wedding receptions, banquets, and fancy dinners during the '50s and '60s. The most common origin story says that the chef at Brighton Beach Hotel in New York prepared it one evening for the owners, Mr. and Mrs. King, and it was so well received that it was quickly added to the hotel's menu.

INGREDIENTS

4 tablespoons (½ stick) unsalted butter

½ cup chopped green bell pepper

½ cup chopped onion

½ cup chopped cremini mushrooms

¼ cup all-purpose flour

1½ cups whole milk

½ cup low-sodium chicken broth

2 cups cubed cooked chicken (see Note)

¼ cup chopped pickled cherry peppers

¼ teaspoon garlic powder

½ teaspoon kosher salt

Freshly ground black pepper

Baguette, cut into four pieces, for serving

DIRECTIONS

1. In a large skillet, melt the butter over medium-high heat. Add the bell pepper and onion and cook, stirring, for about 4 minutes. Add the mushrooms and cook for 2 to 3 minutes more.

2. Add the flour and stir well. While stirring, add the milk and broth. Bring the mixture to a boil while stirring frequently, then reduce the heat to medium-low. Add the chicken, cherry peppers, garlic powder, salt, and black pepper and mix well. Cook, stirring, until the mixture has thickened, about 5 minutes.

3. Serve over baguette.

NOTE

To cook the chicken, place 2 medium boneless, skinless chicken breasts on a baking sheet and bake at 350°F for 30 minutes. Cut into cubes.

Chicken Kiev

Yield: Serves 6 | Prep Time: 30 minutes plus chilling time for herb butter | Cook Time: 20-25 minutes

While there's some dispute about the origins of Chicken Kiev, many credit the Continental Hotel in Kiev with inventing the modern version of the dish in the early 1900s. The dish started to get mentioned in U.S. newspapers in 1937 and became popular nationwide after features in the *New York Times* and *Gourmet* magazine in the late 1940s, when it became a symbol of high-class Soviet cuisine.

INGREDIENTS

½ cup (1 stick) unsalted butter, softened

1½ tablespoons finely chopped fresh tarragon

1½ tablespoons finely chopped fresh chives

1½ tablespoons finely chopped parsley

1½ teaspoons finely chopped fresh thyme

½ teaspoon kosher salt

¼ teaspoon freshly ground black pepper

6 boneless, skinless chicken breasts

1 cup panko bread crumbs

¼ cup grated Parmesan cheese

1 cup all-purpose flour

3 large eggs, beaten

Vegetable oil, for frying

Hot cooked rice, for serving

DIRECTIONS

1. In a small bowl, mix the butter, tarragon, chives, parsley, thyme, salt, and pepper. Scoop the butter onto a piece of plastic wrap or parchment paper and shape into a log. Wrap and place in the freezer until firm, about 2 hours.

2. Slice the butter into 6 equal pieces. Set aside. Pound the chicken between two sheets of plastic wrap to ¼ inch thick.

3. Place a piece of the herb butter in the center of one piece of chicken and fold in the sides to cover fully. Secure with toothpicks. Repeat with the remaining chicken.

4. Preheat the oven to 350°F. Line a baking sheet with aluminum foil.

5. In a small bowl, combine the panko and Parmesan. Put the flour in a separate dish and the eggs in another.

6. One at a time, dredge a chicken roll in the flour, then dip in the egg, and then dredge in the panko mixture. Repeat with the remaining chicken rolls.

7. In a deep skillet, heat ½ to 1 inch of vegetable oil over medium-high heat.

8. Fry 2 or 3 chicken rolls at a time until golden brown on all sides, about 5 minutes.

9. Place on the baking sheet. Bake for 15 to 20 minutes, or until fully cooked. Serve with hot rice.

Beef Wellington

Yield: Serves 2 to 4 | Prep Time: 20 minutes plus 30 minutes chill time | Cook Time: 50-55 minutes

Beef Wellington was President Richard Nixon's favorite meal, which might have been due to its surge in popularity in the 1950s. The beef tenderloin is seared, topped with additional seasonings and prosciutto, and then wrapped up in a blanket of puff pastry.

INGREDIENTS

Duxelles

1 pound white cremini mushrooms

1 shallot, coarsely chopped

4 garlic cloves, coarsely chopped

Leaves from 2 sprigs fresh thyme

1 tablespoon unsalted butter

1 tablespoon olive oil

Kosher salt and freshly ground black pepper

Beef Tenderloin

1 (1-pound) center cut beef tenderloin (filet mignon), trimmed

Kosher salt and freshly ground black pepper

2 tablespoons Dijon mustard

12 thin slices prosciutto

All-purpose flour, for rolling

1 pound puff pastry, thawed if frozen

1 large egg, lightly beaten

DIRECTIONS

1. *For the duxelles:* Place the mushrooms, shallot, garlic, and thyme in a food processor and pulse until finely chopped.

2. In a large skillet, melt the butter with the olive oil over medium heat. Add the mushroom mixture and cook, stirring, for 8 to 10 minutes. Season with salt and pepper and set aside to cool.

3. *For the beef tenderloin:* Season the beef tenderloin with salt and pepper and coat with the mustard. Meanwhile, set out the prosciutto on a sheet of plastic wrap. Shingle the prosciutto so it forms a rectangle that is big enough to encompass the entire piece of beef.

4. Place the beef on the prosciutto. Cover the beef with a layer of the duxelles. Roll up the beef, using the plastic wrap to tie it up nice and tight. Tuck in the ends of the prosciutto as you roll the beef.

5. Roll it up tightly in plastic wrap and twist the ends to seal it completely. Refrigerate for 30 minutes to set.

6. Preheat the oven to 425°F.

7. Lightly flour a work surface. Set the puff pastry on top and roll it out to about a ¼-inch thickness. Remove the beef from the refrigerator and cut off the plastic. Set the beef in the center of the pastry and fold over the longer sides, brushing with the egg wash to seal.

8. Place the beef seam-side down on a baking sheet. Brush the top of the pastry with the egg. Bake for 40 to 45 minutes, until the pastry is golden brown and the beef registers 125°F at the center. Remove from the oven and rest before cutting into thick slices. Serve.

1950s Goulash

Yield: Serves 6 | Prep Time: 10 minutes | Cook Time: 1 hour 5 minutes

The waves of immigration in the early twentieth century brought foods from all around the globe to the American palate. Goulash, a traditional Hungarian dish, was one that resonated with the American public due to its comforting mix of ground beef, pasta, and veggies.

INGREDIENTS

⅓ cup plus 1 tablespoon olive oil

1½ pounds lean ground beef

3 garlic cloves, minced

1 yellow onion, diced

½ cup beef broth

2 (15-ounce) cans tomato sauce

2 (15-ounce) cans diced tomatoes

3 bay leaves

1 tablespoon seasoned salt

1½ teaspoons freshly ground black pepper

1 tablespoon paprika

2 cups uncooked elbow macaroni

DIRECTIONS

1. In a large pot, heat 1 tablespoon of the olive oil over medium-high heat. Add the ground beef and sauté until browned, 8 to 10 minutes.

2. Add the garlic, onion, and remaining ⅓ cup olive oil and cook for 3 to 5 minutes.

3. Add the broth, tomato sauce, diced tomatoes, bay leaves, seasoned salt, pepper, and paprika. Mix well.

4. Reduce the heat to medium-low and cover. Cook for 20 minutes, stirring occasionally.

5. Add the uncooked elbow macaroni. Stir well until everything is combined.

6. Cover once again and simmer for about 30 minutes.

7. Once cooked, remove and discard the bay leaves. Serve.

6

Dessert

In the postwar era, desserts were the flourish at the end of a spectacular dinner. It was a chance to truly get creative in the kitchen, whether by trying out some new recipe found in the latest newspaper or adding a few decorative touches to make the dish really shine. KitchenAid stand mixers were first introduced in the 1920s, providing homemakers with the opportunity to further explore their baking desires, while boxed cake mix came on the market in the 1930s, simplifying the baking process even more. Duncan Hines solidified the trendiness of baking with boxed mixes when he came out with a line in 1952. Dessert no longer had to be a luxury, and I'm certain you'll want to make a few of these recipes any night of the week.

Hummingbird Cake

Yield: Serves 12 to 16 | Prep Time: 15 minutes | Cook Time: 25-28 minutes

County fairs and baking competitions were once resplendent with prized hummingbird cakes. This layered sweet is a marvel to behold, and with cream cheese frosting on top, it's sure to earn praise all around.

INGREDIENTS

Cake

Butter, for the pans

3 cups all-purpose flour, plus more for dusting

2 cups granulated sugar

1 teaspoon kosher salt

1 teaspoon baking powder

1 teaspoon baking soda

1 teaspoon ground cinnamon

¼ teaspoon grated nutmeg

1⅓ cups vegetable oil

2 teaspoons vanilla extract

3 large eggs, lightly beaten

2 cups mashed ripe bananas

1 cup chopped pecans, toasted

1 (8-ounce) can crushed pineapple with juice

Frosting

2 (8-ounce) packages cream cheese, at room temperature

1 cup (2 sticks) unsalted butter, softened

7 cups confectioners' sugar

2 teaspoons vanilla extract

Pinch of kosher salt

1 cup chopped toasted pecans

Halved pecans, for top of cake (optional)

DIRECTIONS

1. *For the cake:* Preheat the oven to 350°F. Grease and flour three 9-inch cake pans.

2. In a large bowl, whisk together the flour, granulated sugar, salt, baking powder, baking soda, cinnamon, and nutmeg.

3. Add the vegetable oil, vanilla, and eggs and stir just to combine.

4. Stir in the mashed banana, pecans, and pineapple just until mixed in.

5. Divide the batter evenly among the prepared cake pans.

6. Bake for 25 to 28 minutes, until a toothpick inserted into the middle comes out clean.

7. Let cool in the pans for 10 to 15 minutes. Carefully remove and place on a wire rack to cool completely.

8. *For the frosting:* In the bowl of a stand mixer fitted with the paddle attachment or in a large bowl using a hand mixer, beat the cream cheese and butter until creamy.

9. Gradually add the confectioners' sugar and beat until fully incorporated and fluffy. Add the vanilla and salt.

10. Place a cake layer on a cake stand or cake plate. Spread ¾ to 1 cup of the frosting between each layer.

11. Spread the top and sides with the remaining frosting.

12. Sprinkle the sides of the cake with the chopped pecans. Top the cake with pecan halves, if desired.

13. Chill the cake for 1 hour before cutting. Serve.

Knickerbocker Glory

Yield: Serves 4 | Prep Time: 5 minutes | Cook Time: N/A

Ice cream became a mainstay for U.S. troops during World War II. Because ice cream was easy to digest, full of calcium, and good for morale, the navy launched a floating ice cream parlor in the western Pacific, and the army supplied enough ingredients to produce about 80 million gallons per year. In fact, the U.S. military was the world's largest ice cream manufacturer in 1943! After the war, Americans' love of ice cream continued to flourish with several chain shops like Dairy Queen and Tastee Freez sprouting up around the country, serving everything from single-scoop cones to fancy Knickerbocker Glories.

INGREDIENTS

1 pint raspberries, rinsed and dried

1 pint blackberries, rinsed and dried

1 cup strawberries, rinsed and chopped

4 cups vanilla ice cream

¼ cup maraschino cherry juice

Whipped topping

Additional fruit for topping

4 cookie straws

4 maraschino cherries

DIRECTIONS

1. Evenly distribute the raspberries, blackberries, and strawberries among four parfait glasses. Top with 1 cup of ice cream each. Pour maraschino cherry juice over each.

2. Top with whipped topping, additional fruit, a cookie straw, and a maraschino cherry. Serve.

VARIATIONS

Use whatever fruit is in season! Peaches and raspberries work great for a melba knickerbocker while blueberries and strawberries make a patriotic knickerbocker.

Pineapple Upside-Down Cake

Yield: Serves 8 to 10 | Prep Time: 15 minutes | Cook Time: 40 minutes, plus 30 minutes cooling time

This soft, sweet cake makes a pretty addition to any post-dinner spread. The contrast between the golden pineapple slices, which grew in popularity after James Dole purchased nearly the entire island of Lanai in Hawaii to transform it into a pineapple farm in the 1920s, and the fiery red maraschino cherries, popularized in the post-Prohibition era after the cherries were stored in a sugar syrup instead of alcohol, catches my eye every time.

INGREDIENTS

6 tablespoons (¾ stick) unsalted butter

¾ cup packed light brown sugar

7–8 slices canned pineapple

14 maraschino cherries

1 cup all-purpose flour

¾ cup granulated sugar

2 teaspoons baking powder

½ teaspoon ground cardamom

Pinch of kosher salt

1 large egg

½ cup buttermilk

⅓ cup sour cream

3 tablespoons vegetable oil

1 teaspoon vanilla extract

1 teaspoon rum extract

DIRECTIONS

1. Preheat the oven to 350°F.

2. In a small bowl, melt the butter in the microwave.

3. Pour the melted butter evenly into a 9-inch springform cake pan set on top of a baking sheet.

4. Sprinkle the brown sugar over the melted butter.

5. Add 5 whole slices of pineapple in the pan. (See photo.)

6. Halve 2 pineapple slices and place them between the whole slices.

7. Place one cherry in the center cut-outs of both the whole and halved slices and in any outside gaps. (See photo.)

8. In a large bowl, whisk together the flour, granulated sugar, baking powder, cardamom, and salt.

9. In a 2-cup liquid measuring cup, whisk together the egg, buttermilk, sour cream, vegetable oil, vanilla, and rum extract.

10. Add the buttermilk mixture to the flour mixture and fold it in with a spatula just until combined. Do not overmix.

11. Carefully pour the batter over the pineapple in the pan.

12. Bake for 40 minutes, or until the cake is set and golden.

13. Place the pan on a wire rack to cool for at least 30 minutes or longer before removing the springform pan ring and inverting onto a cake plate. Slice and serve.

Creamsicle Jell-O Mold

Yield: Serves 10 to 12 | Prep Time: 20 minutes | Chill Time: Overnight

Jell-O molds are an iconic part of the baby boomer era of food. Jell-O had many different appeals. It was budget-friendly, since leftovers would last longer when encased in Jell-O. Plus, it was a tidy dish where guests wouldn't have to worry about leaving crumbs everywhere. This creamy version is an homage to the once-popular dish.

INGREDIENTS

Orange Filling

2 (0.25-ounce) envelopes unflavored gelatin

½ cup cold water

½ cup boiling water

½ cup sugar

2 cups fresh orange juice

Vanilla Base

2 cups vanilla bean ice cream

3 (0.25-ounce) envelopes unflavored gelatin

½ cup cold water

1 cup boiling water

¼ cup sugar

DIRECTIONS

1. *For the orange filling:* In a medium bowl, sprinkle the gelatin over the cold water and set aside for 5 minutes. The gelatin will soften and "bloom." Pour the boiling water over the gelatin and whisk until completely dissolved. Add the sugar and orange juice and stir to dissolve the sugar.

2. Pour into an 8 × 8-inch dish and refrigerate for at least 4 hours, or until firm.

3. *For the vanilla base:* Scoop the ice cream into a large bowl and melt in the microwave, about 2 minutes. Set aside to cool to room temperature.

4. In a medium bowl, sprinkle the gelatin over the cold water and set aside for 5 minutes. The gelatin will soften and "bloom." Pour the boiling water over the gelatin and whisk until completely dissolved. Add the sugar and stir to dissolve. Stir in the melted ice cream.

5. Allow the mixture to rest and return to room temperature.

6. Remove the orange filling from the fridge and cut into cubes. Transfer the cubes to a Jell-O mold of your choice. Gently pour the vanilla mixture over the orange cubes. Carefully shake the mold to release any trapped air pockets. Cover and refrigerate overnight.

7. When ready to serve, fill a large container (or the sink) with hot water. Carefully dip the bottom of the mold into the water for 5 to 10 seconds. This will help release the Jell-O from the mold. Dry the bottom of the mold and invert it over a serving dish.

8. Cut into slices and serve.

Chocolate Cream Pie

Yield: Serves 8 to 10 | Prep Time: 20 minutes | Chill Time: 4 hours

Chocolate cream pies were often found on the menus of local diners in the 1950s and '60s. There'd often be stainless-steel siding and a jukebox in the corner while a freshly made chocolate cream pie sat under a glass dome on the counter.

INGREDIENTS

⅔ cup sugar

¼ cup unsweetened dark cocoa powder

½ teaspoon espresso powder

3 tablespoons cornstarch

¼ teaspoon kosher salt

2¼ cups whole milk

1½ teaspoons vanilla extract

1 refrigerated pie crust, baked according to the package directions

Whipped topping, thawed, for garnish

DIRECTIONS

1. In a medium saucepan, combine the sugar, cocoa powder, espresso powder, cornstarch, and salt. Whisk gently to combine. Set over medium-high heat. While stirring continuously, slowly add the milk and bring to a boil. Remove from the heat and stir in the vanilla.

2. Pour into the pie crust and chill until firm.

3. Dollop the whipped topping over the pie.

4. Refrigerate for 4 hours or until ready to serve.

Holiday Fruit Cake

Yield: 1 loaf | Prep Time: 20 minutes | Cook Time: 2 hours

Fruit cake recipes were typically found in magazines and newspapers back in the '50s and '60s, and the cakes themselves often made an appearance at family holidays when I was growing up. My family loved to make them because they were packed with different fruits, and due to their moisture, they seemed to last around the house for the entire holiday season! While the modern audience doesn't always appreciate a good fruit cake, it's about time they had a comeback.

INGREDIENTS

1 teaspoon baking soda

1 cup sour cream

1 cup chopped dates

1 cup raisins

½ cup glazed red cherries, chopped

½ cup glazed green cherries, chopped

½ cup glazed citron, chopped

1 cup chopped pecans

2 cups all-purpose flour

½ cup (1 stick) unsalted butter, softened

1 cup sugar

1 large egg

1 teaspoon kosher salt

DIRECTIONS

1. Preheat the oven to 325°F. Line a loaf pan with parchment paper. Coat the parchment paper with cooking spray.

2. In a small bowl, mix together the baking soda and sour cream.

3. In another small bowl, combine the dates, raisins, cherries, citron, pecans, and ¼ cup of the flour. Stir gently to coat the fruit and nuts.

4. In a large bowl, beat together the butter and sugar until fluffy and lemony yellow. Mix in the egg until combined, then the salt, followed by the sour cream mixture.

5. Add the remaining 1¾ cups flour in batches, mixing until just combined. Fold in the fruit mixture gently. The batter will be very heavy.

6. Pour the batter into the prepared loaf pan and smooth the top.

7. Bake for 1½ to 2 hours, or until a toothpick inserted into the center comes out clean.

8. Set on a wire rack to cool for 5 minutes. Use the edges of the parchment paper to lift the cake out of the pan. Let cool completely before slicing.

Peanut Brittle

Yield: 24 pieces │ Prep Time: 5 minutes │ Cook Time: 20 minutes

Candy shop sweets have an innocent charm about them that I just love. My husband and I once spent a long weekend up in a small town in Michigan that had the most adorable vintage candy shop, and you better believe I loaded up on the peanut brittle! The Spanish peanuts have a higher oil content than regular peanuts, making them ideal for baking into candies. Be sure to measure and prepare all the ingredients before beginning, as once the candy begins cooking, time is of the essence.

INGREDIENTS

½ cup (1 stick) plus 3 tablespoons unsalted butter, softened

2 cups sugar

1 cup corn syrup

½ cup water

3 cups Spanish peanuts

1 tablespoon vanilla extract

1 tablespoon baking soda

1 teaspoon kosher salt

DIRECTIONS

1. Butter a jelly-roll pan liberally with 3 tablespoons of the butter.

2. In a large heavy-bottomed saucepan, combine the sugar, corn syrup, and water. Attach a candy thermometer and bring the mixture to a boil over medium-high heat. Boil until the mixture reaches 240°F. Stir in the peanuts and cook, stirring, until the candy reaches 280°F to 300°F. (The lower the temperature, the softer the brittle.)

3. Remove the pan from the heat immediately and quickly add the remaining butter, the vanilla, baking soda, and salt. Stir carefully but vigorously only until the butter melts, and then quickly pour the brittle onto the prepared pan. Carefully tip the pan to bring the mixture to all corners. Avoid using a spatula, as the mixture will stick and will have an unpleasant finish. Set aside and allow to cool completely.

4. When the brittle has completely cooled, break into pieces and serve.

Homemade Chocolate *Fudge Candies*

Yield: 24–36 rolls | Prep Time: 30 minutes | Cook Time: 2 hours

There's nothing like enjoying a couple of squares of homemade fudge to satisfy those sweet tooth cravings. This version of fudge tastes remarkably similar to Tootsie Rolls, the individually wrapped candies that children could once buy in candy shops for pennies and nickels out of their allowance. This recipe brings that sweet nostalgic charm back home.

INGREDIENTS

4 tablespoons (½ stick) unsalted butter, plus more for the pan

⅔ cup unsweetened cocoa powder

3 cups sugar

⅛ teaspoon kosher salt

1½ cups whole milk

1 teaspoon vanilla extract

DIRECTIONS

1. Butter a 9-inch square pan. Cut twenty-four to thirty-six 4-inch squares from parchment paper.

2. In a heavy 4-quart saucepan, thoroughly combine the cocoa powder, sugar, and salt.

3. Gradually stir in the milk with a whisk.

4. Bring to a boil over medium heat, stirring continuously. Once the mixture boils, stop stirring.

5. Clip a candy thermometer to the side of the pan, ensuring that the bulb is not sitting on the bottom.

6. Boil, without stirring, until the mixture reaches 230°F (soft ball stage).

7. Remove from the heat and add the butter and vanilla, stirring with a wooden spoon. The mixture will hiss and bubble vigorously when you add these ingredients, so be careful.

8. Pour into the prepared pan and place in the fridge. Once completely cool, remove from the fridge and divide into 24 to 36 equal portions. Roll each piece between your palms into the fudge candy shape. Once shaped, wrap in the prepared parchment squares.

9. Store in an airtight container in the fridge.

Grasshopper Pie

Yield: 1 pie; serves 8 to 10 | Prep Time: 20 minutes | Chill Time: 6 hours

This mint-green chiffon-style pie was a hit in the old-time diner scene. The name is actually borrowed from the mint-flavored cocktail, popularized in the South in the 1950s and '60s, which also features crème de menthe and crème de cacao.

INGREDIENTS

1 (15.25-ounce) package mint creme chocolate sandwich cookies

6 tablespoons (¾ stick) unsalted butter, melted

40 large marshmallows

2⅓ cups heavy cream

¼ cup crème de cacao, clear

¼ cup crème de menthe, green

Vanilla ice cream, for serving

DIRECTIONS

1. Reserve ¼ cup chocolate sandwich cookies, and place the remaining cookies in a food processor and pulse until they are fine crumbs. Put the crumbs into a medium bowl and combine with the melted butter.

2. Pour the crumb mixture into a deep dish 9-inch pie plate and spread it in an even layer over the bottom.

3. Using a large spoon or dry measuring cup, work the crumbs up the sides of the pie plate, creating the crust. Set aside.

4. In a large pot, combine the marshmallows and 1 cup of the heavy cream over medium heat, stirring continuously.

5. Once the marshmallows are completely melted, remove from the heat and pour in the crème de cacao and crème de menthe. Mix thoroughly.

6. Set the marshmallow mixture aside to cool for 10 minutes.

7. While that cools, beat the remaining heavy cream in a large bowl until it holds stiff peaks.

8. Pour one-third of the marshmallow mixture into the whipped cream and fold in.

9. Repeat two more times, until all is incorporated.

10. Pour into the pie shell. Freeze, uncovered, for 1 hour.

11. After 1 hour, cover the pie and freeze until solid, about 5 hours or up to overnight.

12. Pull out the pie 10 minutes before serving. Cut into slices and serve with ice cream and the reserved cookies.

Cinnamon Whiskey Cake

Yield: 1 cake; serves 10 to 12 | Prep Time: 15 minutes | Cook Time: 1 hour

Baking with alcohol saw a resurgence of interest in the '50s and '60s in recipes like Bananas Foster (page 187). I used whiskey instead of rum in this recipe to add a twist to the cake, but you could stick to the traditional version with light rum (a common ingredient in baked goods in the '40s and '50s), experiment with an amber rum for a sweeter flavor, or try a spiced rum for the holidays. Feel free to play around.

INGREDIENTS

1 (8-ounce) package chopped walnuts

1 cup (2 sticks) unsalted butter, softened

1½ cups sugar

½ cup vegetable oil

4 large eggs

2 teaspoons vanilla extract

½ cup cinnamon whiskey

3 cups all-purpose flour

1 (3.4-ounce) package instant vanilla pudding mix

2 teaspoons baking powder

½ teaspoon baking soda

½ teaspoon kosher salt

DIRECTIONS

1. Preheat the oven to 350°F. Generously spray a standard 10-inch Bundt pan with cooking spray.

2. Fill the bottom of the Bundt pan with walnuts.

3. In the bowl of a stand mixer fitted with the paddle attachment, cream the butter and sugar together on medium speed. Stir in the vegetable oil, eggs, vanilla, and whiskey. Add the flour, pudding mix, baking powder, baking soda, and salt and stir until blended. Pour the batter into the Bundt pan on top of the walnuts.

4. Bake for 55 to 60 minutes until a toothpick inserted into the center of the cake comes out clean. Let cool completely before inverting. Cut into slices and serve.

Chocolate Mayonnaise Cake

Yield: 1 cake; serves 10 to 12 | Prep Time: 15 minutes | Cook Time: 35 minutes

I know. As soon as you saw the word "mayonnaise," you started to have some hesitation. I did too, until I remembered that mayonnaise is essentially just a combination of eggs and oil, two ingredients that regularly appear in any cake recipe. Plus, the rising popularity of Miracle Whip in the 1940s and '50s introduced mayonnaise into a slew of new recipes. Its presence here makes the cake moister than ever.

INGREDIENTS

Cake

2 cups all-purpose flour

1 cup granulated sugar

¼ cup unsweetened cocoa powder

2 teaspoons baking soda

1 cup water

1 cup mayonnaise

1 teaspoon vanilla extract

1 tablespoon brewed coffee, black

2 tablespoons French vanilla coffee creamer

Frosting

½ cup packed light brown sugar

4 tablespoons (½ stick) unsalted butter

2 tablespoons French vanilla coffee creamer

2 cups loosely packed confectioners' sugar

Chocolate chips for serving

DIRECTIONS

1. *For the cake:* Preheat the oven to 350°F. Coat an 8 × 8-inch baking dish with cooking spray.

2. In a large bowl, mix together the flour, granulated sugar, cocoa powder, and baking soda.

3. In a separate bowl, whisk together the water, mayonnaise, vanilla, and coffee.

4. Slowly add the coffee mixture to the flour mixture. Stir just until combined and pour into the prepared baking dish.

5. Bake for 30 to 35 minutes, until a toothpick inserted into the center comes out clean.

6. *For the frosting:* In a medium saucepan, combine the brown sugar and butter and cook over medium heat until bubbling, about 5 minutes. Be sure to whisk continuously, so it doesn't burn.

7. Take off the heat and stir in the creamer. Then gradually add the confectioners' sugar and whisk until smooth.

8. Frost the cake, cut into slices, and serve, garnished with chocolate chips.

Lemon Chiffon Cake

Yield: 1 cake; serves 10 to 12 | Prep Time: 20 minutes | Cook Time: 1 hour

Chiffon cakes were all the rage in the 1950s. Harry Baker, a California insurance agent, is credited with inventing the original chiffon cake, which becomes so light and airy because of the separation of the egg whites from the yolks and the use of vegetable oil rather than butter or shortening. It's an ideal dessert recipe for spring and summer.

INGREDIENTS

Lemon Cake

2 cups all-purpose flour

1½ cups granulated sugar

1 tablespoon baking powder

½ teaspoon kosher salt

½ cup vegetable oil

8 large eggs, separated

2½ tablespoons grated lemon zest

¼ cup fresh lemon juice

Lemon Glaze

6 tablespoons (¾ stick) unsalted butter, melted

2 tablespoons lemon zest

3 tablespoons fresh lemon juice

2 cups confectioners' sugar

1 teaspoon vanilla extract

Lemon slices, for garnish

DIRECTIONS

1. *For the lemon cake:* Preheat the oven to 325°F.

2. In a large bowl, stir together the flour, granulated sugar, baking powder, and salt. Add the vegetable oil, egg yolks, lemon zest, lemon juice, and ¼ cup water and whisk until well combined.

3. In another large bowl, beat the egg whites until they hold stiff peaks. Fold one-third of the whipped egg whites into the flour batter to lighten. Gently fold in the remaining egg whites until the mixture is combined; do not overmix or the batter will deflate. Pour into an ungreased 8-inch Bundt pan; tap gently on the counter to release air pockets.

4. Bake for 50 to 60 minutes, or until the cake springs back when touched. Invert the Bundt pan immediately after removing from the oven and allow to cool completely, then remove from the pan.

5. *For the lemon glaze:* In a medium bowl, combine the butter, lemon zest, lemon juice, confectioners' sugar, and vanilla, and stir until smooth. Pour over the cooled cake and spread with a spatula. The glaze will set hard within 30 minutes. Add a layer of lemon slices and drizzle additional glaze on top, if desired. Cut into slices and serve.

Baked Alaska

Yield: Serves 8 | Prep Time: 30 minutes plus overnight chilling time | Cook Time: 35 minutes

Some recipes remind us that baking is as much an art form as a practical endeavor. Flaming food was considered a glamorous hobby. It may take a bit of practice to get the swirled topping just right, but it's just another excuse to make it again!

INGREDIENTS

2 cups strawberry ice cream

2 cups chocolate ice cream

2 cups vanilla ice cream

Brownie Base

1 (15.25-ounce) box brownie mix

Vegetable oil and eggs as needed for the brownie mix

Meringue Frosting

3 large egg whites

Pinch of cream of tartar

⅔ cup sugar

Pinch or two of kosher salt

1 teaspoon vanilla extract

DIRECTIONS

1. Coat a 1.5-quart bowl (the rim should be about 9 inches in diameter) lightly with cooking spray. Line with two pieces of plastic wrap, overlapping them in the center. There should be plenty of overhang.

2. Scoop the ice cream into the bowl in any pattern you wish. Use the overhanging plastic wrap to cover the exposed ice cream and press it mostly flat. Place this ice cream bowl in the freezer for 3 to 6 hours, or overnight, until fully firm again.

3. *For the brownie base:* Preheat the oven to 350°F. Prepare the brownie mix in a 9-inch cake pan, according to package directions. Let cool for 15 minutes, then flip onto a rack. Put the rack with the brownie in the freezer to firm up for about 30 minutes.

4. Using the ice cream bowl to measure, cut away any excess brownie. Use the plastic covering the mold as handles to yank the firm ice cream out of the bowl and onto the brownie. Return the ice cream–topped brownie cake to the freezer to firm again for 1 to 2 hours.

5. *For the meringue frosting:* In the bowl of a stand mixer fitted with the whisk attachment, beat the egg whites with the cream of tartar on low speed until satiny peaks form and then beat in the sugar a spoonful at a time. Beat in the salt and vanilla.

6. Frost the cake by spreading the meringue in big, messy swirls on top. Return the cake to the freezer for another hour or up to overnight.

7. Remove from the freezer and toast the tops of the meringue peaks with a blow torch to achieve golden peaks.

Magic Tomato Soup Cupcakes

Yield: 12 cupcakes | Prep Time: 15 minutes | Cook Time: 20-22 minutes

Yes, there's actually tomato soup in these. Canned soups were used in all sorts of recipes as convenient shortcuts in magazine ads in the 1950s, and that included desserts. Think of this as a shortcut to the holiday-favorite spice cake. No one will even know your secret ingredient unless you decide to point it out.

INGREDIENTS

Cupcakes

2¼ cups all-purpose flour

¾ cup granulated sugar

¾ cup lightly packed light brown sugar

1½ teaspoons ground cinnamon

¼ teaspoon ground allspice

¼ teaspoon grated nutmeg

½ teaspoon baking soda

¼ teaspoon kosher salt

1 cup (2 sticks) unsalted butter, melted and warm

3 large eggs

1 (10¾-ounce) can tomato soup

½ cup hot water

Frosting

1 (7-ounce) container Marshmallow Fluff

½ (8-ounce) package cream cheese, softened

1 (8-ounce) tub frozen whipped topping

DIRECTIONS

1. *For the cupcakes:* Preheat the oven to 350°F. Line a cupcake pan with paper liners.

2. In a large bowl, whisk together the flour, granulated sugar, brown sugar, cinnamon, allspice, nutmeg, baking soda, and salt. In a separate bowl, whisk together the butter and eggs. Add the butter mixture into the flour mixture and whisk to combine. Add the tomato soup and whisk to combine. Add ¼ cup of the hot water and whisk to combine. Pour in the remaining hot water and whisk to combine.

3. Fill the cupcake liners three-quarters of the way up and bake for 20 to 22 minutes or until a toothpick inserted into the center comes out clean and the cupcake springs back when gently pressed. Transfer the cupcakes to a wire rack to cool completely before frosting.

4. *For the frosting:* In the bowl of a stand mixer fitted with the whisk attachment, combine the Fluff and cream cheese and beat on medium speed until combined. Turn off the mixer and stir in the frozen whipped topping.

5. Transfer the frosting to a pastry bag fitted with your preferred tip and pipe the frosting onto the cupcakes. Serve.

Harvey Wallbanger Cake

Yield: 1 cake; serves 10 to 12 | Prep Time: 15 minutes | Cook Time: 40-45 minutes

Similar to the Grasshopper Pie (page 171), here's another dessert inspired by a popular mixed drink of the same name. Donato "Duke" Antone, owner of the Los Angeles bar Blackwatch, named the drink after an imaginary surfer character who had a tendency to start bumping into the walls after imbibing several drinks. The Galliano and orange juice carried over from the drink to the cake, and the glaze helps put this cake right over the edge.

INGREDIENTS

Cake

1 (18.5-ounce) box yellow cake mix

1 (3.5-ounce) package instant vanilla pudding mix

4 large eggs

1 cup vegetable oil

½ cup Galliano liqueur

¾ cup fresh orange juice

Glaze

¾ cup confectioners' sugar

1 tablespoon orange zest

1–2 tablespoons fresh orange juice

Lemon slices, for garnish (optional)

DIRECTIONS

1. *For the cake*: Preheat the oven to 350°F. Coat a 10-cup Bundt pan with cooking spray.

2. In a large bowl, combine the cake mix, vanilla pudding mix, eggs, oil, liqueur, and orange juice. With a hand mixer, beat for 4 minutes. Pour into the prepared pan and bake for 40 to 45 minutes, or until a toothpick inserted into the center of the cake comes out clean.

3. *For the glaze*: In a small bowl, mix together the confectioners' sugar, orange zest, and orange juice until smooth.

4. When the cake is cooled, invert it onto a serving plate and drizzle with the glaze. Garnish with the lemon slices, if desired.

5. Cut into slices and serve.

Raspberry Jelly Roll

Yield: Serves 8 to 10 | Prep Time: 15 minutes | Cook Time: 15 minutes, plus 40-60 minutes chilling time

Cake rolls are such a fun twist on traditional cake recipes. Home cooks loved to experiment with cake forms in the '50s, from Bundt cakes to cake rolls to loaf cakes and more. I like to mix up the kind of preserves I put in the middle. Sometimes I'll do strawberry, sometimes peach or grape, but raspberry gives it a beautiful deep red hue that looks lovely when presented to guests.

INGREDIENTS

3 large eggs

1 cup granulated sugar

⅓ cup water

1 teaspoon vanilla extract

¾ cup all-purpose flour

1 teaspoon baking powder

¼ teaspoon kosher salt

Confectioners' sugar, for dusting

⅔ cup spreadable raspberry jelly/jam (or any other filling of your choice)

DIRECTIONS

1. Preheat the oven to 375°F. Line a baking sheet with parchment paper or aluminum foil. Coat with cooking spray.

2. In a small bowl, beat the eggs with a hand mixer on high speed for about 5 minutes, or until very thick and lemon colored. Gradually beat in the granulated sugar. Reduce the speed to low and beat in the water and vanilla. Add the flour, baking powder, and salt, beating just until the batter is smooth. Pour into the prepared baking dish, spreading it out well to form a thin, even layer.

3. Bake for 12 to 15 minutes, until a toothpick inserted into the center comes out clean.

4. Spread a clean kitchen towel on your work surface and sprinkle some confectioners' sugar on it. Loosen the edges of the cake, then turn the whole pan upside down onto the towel. Carefully remove the paper from the top. Trim off the hard edges of the cake, and while it's hot, carefully roll the cake lengthwise in the towel from one end to the other. Keep the roll as tight as possible, but apply very little pressure to minimize cracks. Refrigerate the rolled cake for 40 minutes to 1 hour.

5. Remove the cake from the fridge, unroll it gently, and remove the towel. Whisk the raspberry jelly slightly to soften; it's better to use a spreadable jelly. Spread evenly over the cake. Roll it back up and sprinkle more confectioners' sugar on top. Cut into slices and serve.

Bananas Foster

Yield: Serves 2 | Prep Time: 2 minutes | Cook Time: 5 minutes

Bananas Foster was first made in 1951 in New Orleans at a restaurant called Brennan's. The city served as a major port for bananas coming in from South America, so chefs in that area got the freshest inventory to use when experimenting for their menus.

INGREDIENTS

4 tablespoons (½ stick) salted butter

½ cup packed dark brown sugar

¼ cup heavy cream

2 whole bananas, sliced on an angle into thick slices

½ cup dark or light rum

Dash of ground cinnamon

Vanilla ice cream, for serving

DIRECTIONS

1. In a heavy skillet, melt the butter over medium-high heat. Add the brown sugar and stir together. Add the heavy cream and cook for 5 minutes, then stir in the bananas. The mixture should be bubbling.

2. Pour in the rum and stir to combine. Carefully (see Note) use a very long kitchen match or grill lighter to ignite the alcohol in the pan, then let the mixture flame for 30 seconds or so. (It should go out on its own.) You can shake the pan a bit to get it to calm down. Remove from the heat and stir in the cinnamon.

3. Pour the sauce over the vanilla ice cream and serve.

NOTE

This recipe involves igniting alcohol, so be warned and exercise extreme caution!

Hot Milk Cake

Yield: 1 cake; serves 10 to 12 | Prep Time: 15 minutes | Cook Time: 1 hour 10 minutes

Who says you can't make a top-quality cake using basic ingredients? This soft, fluffy cake originated in the Great Depression and was popular for several decades after. It can be dressed up in so many different ways, you may never wind up eating it the same way twice! Top it with whipped cream, sprinkle your favorite berries on top, or drizzle some hot fudge over everything. The possibilities are endless.

INGREDIENTS

½ cup (1 stick) unsalted butter, plus more for greasing the pan

2 cups all-purpose flour, plus more for dusting

1 cup whole milk

2 teaspoons vanilla extract

4 large eggs, room temperature

2 cups granulated sugar

2 teaspoons baking powder

1 teaspoon kosher salt

Confectioners' sugar and raspberries, for garnish

DIRECTIONS

1. Adjust an oven rack to the middle position. Preheat the oven to 325°F. Grease and flour a 12-cup tube pan or Bundt pan.

2. In a small saucepan, melt the butter over low heat. Stir in the milk and vanilla and heat until small bubbles form around the outside of the pan and the mixture is very hot but not boiling, about 5 minutes. Reduce the heat to low.

3. Meanwhile, in the bowl of a stand mixer fitted with the whisk attachment, combine the eggs and sugar and beat on medium-high speed for 5 minutes.

4. In a separate medium bowl, sift together the flour, baking powder, and salt.

5. Once the egg and sugar mixture has tripled in volume, slowly add the hot milk mixture, mixing on low speed until incorporated. Add the flour mixture in two batches, mixing after each addition until just incorporated.

6. Pour the batter into the prepared pan and bake for 1 hour, checking 5 minutes prior to the baking end time. A toothpick inserted into the middle of the cake should come out clean with just a few crumbs attached; do not overbake.

7. Let cool in the pan for 10 minutes before inverting onto a wire rack or serving plate to cool completely. Cut into slices and serve with confectioners' sugar and raspberries.

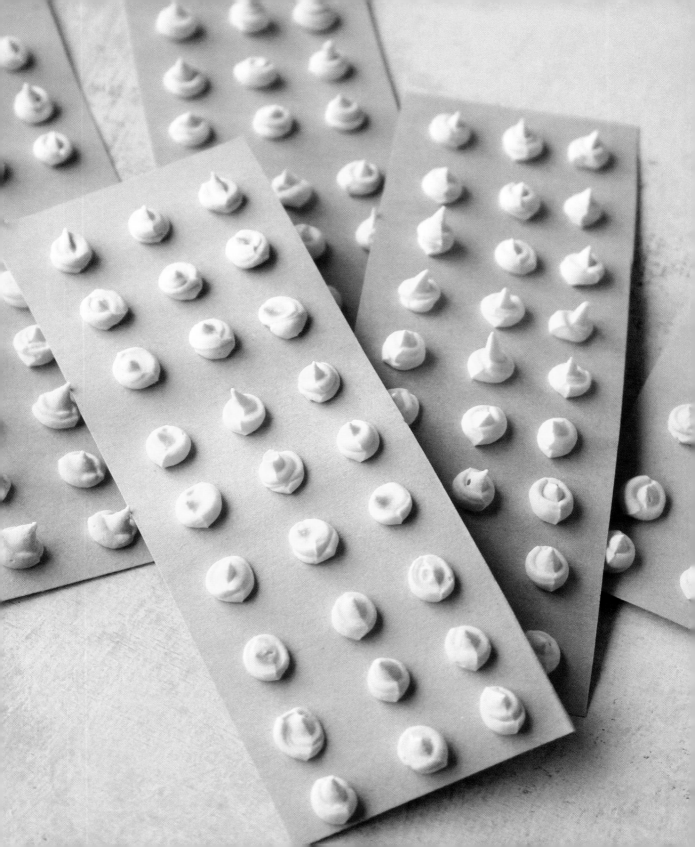

Homemade Candy Buttons

Yield: 8 strips | Prep Time: 10 minutes | Cooling Time: Overnight

I loved eating candy buttons when I was a kid. My family used to play board games during the holidays, like Bingo and Scrabble, and whenever someone won a game, we'd get to pick a prize from my grandmother's secret stash. I'd load up on the rolls of candy buttons, which she always kept handy.

INGREDIENTS

3 tablespoons meringue powder

4 cups confectioners' sugar

6 tablespoons water, plus more as needed

½ teaspoon vanilla, cherry, or any flavored extract

Food coloring

DIRECTIONS

1. In a large bowl, beat together the meringue powder, confectioners' sugar, water, and vanilla (or flavored extract) until the mixture holds stiff peaks and loses its sheen (about 10 minutes). Divide into separate containers, depending on how many colors you plan to use. Mix in the food coloring with rubber spatulas, starting with 3 drops and adding more until you reach your desired color. Keep covered until ready to use.

2. Prepare piping bags with small round tips. Place each color of icing into its own bag. Pipe dots onto strips of paper. Let stand for 2 minutes, then carefully set aside to dry completely. Allow the dots to dry in the open air overnight. Cut the strips into sections and serve.

Old-Time Popcorn Balls

Yield: 12 popcorn balls | Prep Time: 10 minutes | Cook Time: 20 minutes

Popcorn balls seem to be an elementary school tradition. I remember coming home from school one day and telling my mom about how we needed to make a treat to share with the class. She suggested we make popcorn balls because that's what she and her mom used to make for her school events. To this day, I smile when I think of the bond we all share over these sticky, crunchy snacks.

INGREDIENTS

1 teaspoon vegetable oil

1 cup popcorn kernels (to yield about 15 cups popped popcorn)

2 cups sugar

1 cup water

½ cup light corn syrup

2 tablespoons molasses

½ teaspoon vanilla extract

1½ teaspoons kosher salt

Unsalted butter, for hands

DIRECTIONS

1. In a large pot, heat the oil over medium-high heat. Once hot, add the popcorn kernels and place the lid on the pot. Increase the heat to high and shake the pot occasionally until all the kernels have popped. Remove from the heat.

2. In a small saucepan, combine the sugar, water, and corn syrup. Increase the heat to high and boil the sugar mixture until a candy thermometer reads 250°F (hard ball stage). This will take 15 to 20 minutes. If you don't have a candy thermometer, just boil the sugar for 20 minutes and then proceed.

3. When the sugar mixture reaches the hard ball stage, remove from the heat and stir in the molasses and vanilla. Pour this over the popcorn and toss well. Sprinkle the salt over the popcorn and toss well again. Set aside until cool enough to handle.

4. Lay out a long piece of waxed paper on your counter. With buttered hands, form the popcorn into balls and line up on the waxed paper. They might appear to fall apart at first, but cup them with your hands until a tight ball has formed.

5. Repeat with the remaining popcorn. The popcorn balls will keep for up to a week in a sealed plastic container.

Crispy Rice Treats

Yield: 12 crispy rice treats | Prep Time: 15 minutes | Cook Time: 10 minutes

The Kellogg Company first marketed Rice Krispies as a breakfast cereal in 1928 and added melted marshmallows to create Rice Krispies Treats in 1933. The snack version really took off after Alex Doumak came up with a way to speed up and standardize the marshmallow production process in 1948. Kellogg started investing in TV advertising in the 1950s, going so far as sponsoring television shows for children and adults until the FCC ruled against it in 1969. Throughout the '50s and '60s, these soft yet crispy treats were household staples.

INGREDIENTS

½ cup (1 stick) unsalted butter

2 (10-ounce) bags mini marshmallows

½ teaspoon kosher salt (optional)

6 cups crispy rice cereal

DIRECTIONS

1. Line a 9 × 9-inch baking dish with aluminum foil. Coat the foil with cooking spray.

2. In a large pot, melt the butter over medium-low heat. Add 6 cups of the mini marshmallows and the salt (if using). Stir continuously until marshmallows have melted.

3. Remove from the heat and stir in the crispy rice cereal. Stir until just barely coated in the marshmallow mixture. Stir in the remaining mini marshmallows.

4. Pour the mixture into the baking dish and press evenly into the pan.

5. Allow to cool completely before cutting into squares. Serve.

Favorite Carrot Cake

Yield: 1 cake; serves 10 to 12 | Prep Time: 20 minutes | Cook Time: 35 minutes plus 10 minutes cooling time

Carrot cake really started gaining steam in the United States after World War II, but it wasn't until the late '60s that carrot cake and cream cheese frosting became an inseparable combination. You can choose to frost it for dessert or serve without for breakfast or an afternoon snack; this moist cake will be a treat either way.

INGREDIENTS

Butter, for greasing the pans

2½ cups all-purpose flour, plus more for dusting

1½ teaspoons baking soda

1¼ teaspoons baking powder

½ teaspoon kosher salt

2 cups sugar

4 large eggs

1 cup vegetable oil

1 teaspoon vanilla extract

2 cups grated carrots

¾ cup chopped pecans

1 (8-ounce) can pineapple chunks, drained

¾ cup sweetened shredded coconut

1–2 (16-ounce) tubs cream cheese frosting

DIRECTIONS

1. Preheat the oven to 350°F. Line the bottoms of three 8-inch or two 9-inch round cake pans with waxed or parchment paper. Grease the pans with butter and dust with flour.

2. In a large bowl, combine the flour, baking soda, baking powder, and salt with a whisk for 30 seconds. Set aside.

3. In another large bowl, combine the sugar, eggs, vegetable oil, and vanilla. Using a hand mixer, mix for 2 to 3 minutes on medium speed until well blended and light colored.

4. With a spoon, stir in the flour mixture until moistened, then add the carrots, pecans, pineapple, and coconut. Pour into the cake pans.

5. Bake for 35 minutes, or until a toothpick inserted into the center comes out clean.

6. Let the cake layers cool in the pans on a wire rack for 10 minutes, then turn them out of the pans. Let cool completely before frosting. You can use orange frosting and parsley to make carrot decorations, if desired. Cut into slices and serve.

Easy Strawberry Shortcake

Yield: Serves 6 | Prep Time: 15 minutes | Cook Time: 15 minutes

The refrigerator era of cooking offered the opportunity for home cooks to make recipes that they'd normally only get at restaurants, like strawberry shortcake. Dairy products were more readily used now that they could be properly stored.

INGREDIENTS

1½ cups all-purpose flour

2½ teaspoons baking powder

½ teaspoon baking soda

2 tablespoons granulated sugar

½ teaspoon kosher salt

Zest of 1 lemon

½ cup (1 stick) cold unsalted butter

½ cup buttermilk

2 tablespoons coarse sugar

1 (15-ounce) can refrigerated whipped cream

3 cups fresh sliced strawberries

DIRECTIONS

1. Preheat the oven to 425°F. Line a baking sheet with parchment paper.

2. Combine the flour, baking powder, baking soda, granulated sugar, salt, and lemon zest in a small bowl (or food processor).

3. Add the butter and cut it in with a fork or pastry cutter or pulse a few times with a food processor until you have coarse crumbs. Stir in the buttermilk.

4. Drop the dough onto the baking sheet. Sprinkle with coarse sugar and lemon zest. Bake for 15 minutes or until lightly browned.

5. Cut the biscuits in half and spoon some of the whipped cream in between each half. Serve with fresh strawberries.

Cherries Jubilee

Yield: Serves 4 | Prep Time: 5 minutes | Cook Time: 10 minutes

Once you've mastered Bananas Foster (page 187), you'll have no trouble trying out another flaming dessert, like Cherries Jubilee. It's a dish that was made to impress at fancy restaurants, so if you've got in-laws or out-of-town guests you're looking to please, this might just be the dessert to serve.

INGREDIENTS

3 tablespoons unsalted butter

¼ cup sugar

1 pound frozen cherries

Zest and juice of 1 lemon

3 ounces Grand Marnier

Vanilla ice cream, for serving

DIRECTIONS

1. In a medium pan, melt the butter over medium heat. Add the sugar and stir to combine with the butter. Cook until the sugar melts, making a light golden color, 4 to 5 minutes.

2. Add the cherries. Cook, stirring, just until they soften and release their juices, about 5 minutes. Stir in the lemon zest and lemon juice.

3. Turn off the burner. Light a long kitchen or fireplace match, then drizzle the Grand Marnier over the cherries. Hold the match carefully near the edge of the pan to ignite the liqueur, then allow it to burn off (see Note).

4. Spoon the flambéed cherries over scoops of ice cream and serve immediately.

NOTE

This recipe involves igniting alcohol, so be warned and exercise extreme caution!

Classic Peanut Butter Cookies

Yield: 30 cookies | Prep Time: 20 minutes plus 3 hours chilling time | Cook Time: 11 minutes

One of my earliest cooking memories is standing on a tiny stool and pressing a fork into peanut butter cookie dough, working slowly and steadily to make sure the criss-crosses were just perfect. This old-fashioned favorite is still one of my most beloved cookies.

INGREDIENTS

1 cup (2 sticks) unsalted butter, softened

1 cup granulated sugar, plus more for rolling

¾ cup packed light brown sugar

2 large eggs, at room temperature

2 teaspoons vanilla extract

1¼ cups creamy peanut butter

3 cups plus 2 tablespoons all-purpose flour

1 teaspoon baking soda

1 teaspoon baking powder

½ teaspoon kosher salt

DIRECTIONS

1. Preheat the oven to 350°F. Line two large baking sheets with parchment paper or silicone baking mats.

2. In a large bowl using a hand mixer or in the bowl of a stand mixer fitted with the paddle attachment, cream together the butter, granulated sugar, and brown sugar on medium speed until smooth. Add the eggs and mix on high until combined, about 1 minute. Scrape down the sides and bottom of the bowl as needed. Add the vanilla and peanut butter and mix on high until combined.

3. Add the flour, baking soda, baking powder, and salt and mix on low until combined. The dough will be thick and very sticky.

4. Using a 2-inch ice cream scoop, scoop the dough and place on the prepared baking sheets 2 inches apart. Press a fork into the tops to create a criss-cross pattern. Bake for 11 minutes, or until very lightly browned on the sides. The centers will look very soft and undercooked. Remove from the oven and let cool on the baking sheets for 5 minutes before transferring to a wire rack to cool completely, about 10 minutes. The cookies will continue to "set" on the baking sheet during this time. Serve once cooled.

7

Drinks

It's impossible to talk about the infamous cocktail parties of the
'50s and '60s without mentioning the thread that held them
all together: the mixed drinks. I love making recipes like these
when I'm expecting company because their nostalgic appeal
gets everyone so animated. So stock up your liquor cabinet
and roll up your sleeves—it's time to play bartender! And of
course, there are some nonalcoholic concoctions, too.

Chocolate Malt Milk Shake

Yield: Serves 2 | Prep Time: 5 minutes | Cook Time: N/A

When I think of milk shakes, my mind automatically jumps to images of chrome-plated counter-tops and leather swivel chairs while rock 'n' roll music plays softly in the background. No matter how old I get, I'll always find the image of a chocolate malted milk shake endlessly charming.

INGREDIENTS

½ cup chocolate malted milk balls, plus extra for garnish

2 cups chocolate malt frozen custard

½ cup whole milk

2 tablespoons chocolate syrup (optional)

Whipped cream, for garnish

DIRECTIONS

1. In a high-powered blender, grind the chocolate malted milk balls until no large chunks remain. Add the frozen custard and milk (and chocolate syrup for added chocolate flavor, if desired). Blend until you have a smooth, creamy shake.

2. Pour into glasses and garnish with whipped cream and chocolate malted milk balls. Serve.

Shirley Temple

Yield: Serves 1 | Prep Time: 2 minutes | Cook Time: N/A

This used to be my go-to drink as a kid whenever I'd go with my parents to a wedding and there was an open bar. (My brother would get the Roy Rogers.) I used to think that Shirley Temple herself must have done the same, and that's why the drink was named after her, but I've since learned that not only did she not invent the drink, she didn't even like it!

INGREDIENTS

½ cup orange juice

½ cup ginger ale

½ cup lime soda

2 tablespoons grenadine

Wheels of lime and lemon and slices of orange, for garnish

Maraschino cherries with stems, for garnish

DIRECTIONS

1. Fill a large glass half full with ice cubes.

2. Pour the orange juice into the glass, followed by the ginger ale, then the lime soda, and finally the grenadine.

3. Add a lime wheel, a lemon wheel, an orange slice, and maraschino cherries to the beverage.

4. Serve un-stirred, but stir before drinking.

Old Fashioned

Yield: 1 drink | Prep Time: 3-5 minutes | Cook Time: N/A

Cocktail parties were all the rage in the '50s, and while the variety of appetizers from Rumaki (page 45) to a Party Cheese Ball (page 29) often took center stage, it's impossible to have cocktail parties without *Mad Men*–era cocktails, like this classic!

INGREDIENTS

2 ounces bourbon (or rye)

1½ teaspoons simple syrup (see Note)

2–3 dashes Angostura bitters, to taste

Ice

1 orange slice

3 Luxardo cherries

DIRECTIONS

Combine the bourbon, simple syrup, and bitters in a glass and stir to combine. Add the ice, then add the orange slice and Luxardo cherries. Let the drink sit for a few minutes or give it a little shake to let the flavors of the orange and cherries seep into the bourbon. Drink and enjoy.

NOTE

To make a simple syrup, simply bring equal parts water and sugar to a boil, and stir until the sugar has dissolved.

Manhattan

Yield: 1 drink │ Prep Time: 2 minutes │ Cook Time: N/A

Originally emerging from the Manhattan Club in the late nineteenth century to honor Mayor Samuel Tilden, who was running for president, Manhattans made their way into the cultural zeitgeist in full force during the '50s and '60s.

INGREDIENTS

2½ ounces bourbon whiskey

1 ounce sweet vermouth

2 dashes Angostura bitters

Ice

Maraschino cherries

DIRECTIONS

1. In a large mixing glass, combine the bourbon whiskey, sweet vermouth, bitters, and a handful of ice. Stir well until the ingredients are combined and chilled.

2. Strain into a chilled cocktail glass. Garnish with a few maraschino cherries.

Vodka Gimlet

Yield: 1 drink | Prep Time: 2 minutes | Cook Time: N/A

The sweet yet tart edge on this homemade cocktail gives the drink a memorable flair. Feel free to add a garnish of lime for the perfect finishing touch.

INGREDIENTS

Ice cubes

1½ ounces vodka

1 ounce fresh lime juice

1 ounce simple syrup (see Note)

Lime wheel or lime zest, for garnish (optional)

DIRECTIONS

1. Fill a cocktail shaker with ice.

2. Add the vodka, lime juice, and simple syrup.

3. Shake rapidly for about 20 seconds.

4. Strain into a glass filled with ice.

5. Add a lime wheel for garnish, if desired.

NOTE

To make a simple syrup, simply bring equal parts water and sugar to a boil, and stir until the sugar has dissolved.

Whiskey Milk Punch

Yield: 1 drink | Prep Time: 2 minutes | Cook Time: 2 minutes

The first time I tried a Whiskey Milk Punch, I was at a 1950s theme party with a few of my friends. We all got dressed up in decade-appropriate garb and tried out different cocktails and mixed drinks of the time. I was skeptical about mixing alcohol and milk, but somehow, it just works!

INGREDIENTS

2 ounces blended whiskey

1 teaspoon confectioners' sugar

8 ounces whole milk

Ice cubes

Grated nutmeg

Cinnamon sticks, for serving

DIRECTIONS

In a large mixing glass, combine the blended whiskey, confectioners' sugar, milk, and ice cubes. Shake and strain into a glass. Sprinkle the nutmeg on top and serve with a cinnamon stick.

Mint Julep

Yield: 1 drink | Prep Time: 2 minutes | Cook Time: 5 minutes plus 1 hour chilling time

The mint julep drink has been closely associated with the Kentucky Derby since 1938 and became a signature drink for socializing throughout the 1950s and '60s, particularly in the South.

INGREDIENTS

1 large bunch mint leaves, plus 1 additional sprig mint leaves

1 ounce simple syrup (see Note)

2½ ounces bourbon

Ice cubes

Crushed ice

DIRECTIONS

1. Place the bunch of mint leaves in an old mason jar (or other heatproof container) and pour the syrup over the leaves. Place the jar in the fridge and let the leaves steep in the syrup for at least 1 hour. Strain the leaves from the liquid and set the syrup aside.

2. Place mint leaves in a cocktail shaker and pour in the bourbon as well as 1 ounce of the mint-infused simple syrup. Top with a few ice cubes and stir. Fill a chilled silver cup about halfway with ice. Strain the liquid from the cocktail shaker into the cup. Pack crushed ice on top of the liquid to the top of the glass. Garnish the drink with a sprig of mint leaves and serve.

NOTE

To make a simple syrup, simply bring equal parts water and sugar to a boil, and stir until the sugar has dissolved.

Tom Collins

Yield: 1 drink | Prep Time: 2 minutes | Cook Time: N/A

John Collins, a headwaiter at Limmer's Hotel and Coffee House in London, is credited with the invention of both the John Collins and Tom Collins drinks. The John Collins is typically produced using American whiskey while the Tom Collins is usually now made with London Dry Gin, since Old Tom sweetened gin stopped production in the 1960s.

INGREDIENTS

2 sugar cubes

2 ounces gin

1 ounce fresh lemon juice

Ice cubes

Splash of club soda

1 lemon wheel

1 maraschino cherry

DIRECTIONS

Drop the sugar cubes into a tall glass. Add the gin and lemon juice. Stir. Add plenty of ice, and top with a healthy splash of club soda. Garnish with a lemon wheel and maraschino cherry. Serve.

Acknowledgments

Thank you to the incredibly talented chefs who inspired many of these recipes that we now love today. Thank you to the bold women who began cooking in the home and later shared their recipes and passion with the world. Julia Child and Duncan Hines have made cooking possible for so many with their accessible cooking styles, while the Betty Crocker cookbooks have been the country's signature introduction to the culinary world. These pioneers created delicious and inspiring meals for all to learn from and have paved the way for future generations of cooks.

Thank you to Adriana, my best friend and sister, who loves Jell-O more than I do. Thank you for your continuous love and support. Your drive, wit, and intelligence inspire me daily.

Thank you to my incredible culinary and creative team at Prime Publishing, including Megan Von Schönhoff, my wonderful photographer; Tom Krawczyk, my photographer and videographer; Chris Hammond, Judith Hines, and Marlene Stolfo, my culinary test kitchen geniuses; Bryn Clark and Jessica Thelander, my word masters and editors; and Kara Rota, my amazing editor and friend. This book was a team effort, filled with collaboration and creativity that reached no limits.

Index

About the Author

After receiving her master's in culinary arts at Auguste Escoffier in Avignon, France, Addie stayed in France to learn from Christian Etienne at his three-Michelin-star restaurant. Upon leaving France, she spent the next several years working with restaurant groups. She worked in the kitchen for Daniel Boulud and moved coast to coast with Thomas Keller building a career in management, restaurant openings, and brand development. She later joined Martha Stewart Living Omnimedia, where she worked with the editorial team as well as in marketing and sales. While living in New York, Addie completed her bachelor's degree in organizational behavior. Upon leaving New York, Addie joined gravitytank, an innovation consultancy in Chicago. As a culinary designer at gravitytank, Addie designed new food products for companies, large and small. She created edible prototypes for clients and research participants to taste and experience, some of which you may see in stores today. In 2015, she debuted on the Food Network, where she competed on *Cutthroat Kitchen*, and won!

Addie is the executive producer for RecipeLion. Addie oversees and creates culinary content for multiple web platforms and communities, leads video strategy, and oversees the production of in-print books. Addie is passionate about taking easy recipes and making them elegant, without making them complicated. From fine dining to entertaining, to innovation and test kitchens, Addie's experience with food makes these recipes unique and delicious.

Addie and her husband live in Lake Forest, Illinois, with their baby boy and happy puppy, Paisley. Addie is actively involved with youth culinary programs in the Chicagoland area, serving on the board of a bakery and catering company that employs at-risk youth. She is a healthy-food teacher for first-graders in a low-income school district, and aside from eating and entertaining with friends and family, she loves encouraging kids to be creative in the kitchen!